Should Business and Nonbusiness Accounting Be Different?

SHOULD BUSINESS AND

NONBUSINESS ACCOUNTING

BE DIFFERENT?

Robert N. Anthony

Ross Graham Walker Professor
of Management Control (Emeritus)
Harvard Business School

Harvard Business School Press
Boston, Massachusetts

The paper used in this publication meets the requirements of the American
National Standard for Permanence of Paper for Printed Library Materials
Z39.49-1984
Printed in the United States of America

93 92 91 90 89   5 4 3 2 1

Library of Congress Cataloging–in–Publication Data

Anthony, Robert Newton, 1916-
    Should business and nonbusiness accounting be different? / Robert N.
Anthony.
        p.   cm.
        Bibliography: p. 115
        ISBN 0-87584-212-7
        1. Accounting—Standards—United States. 2. Corporations—Accounting
—Standards—United States. 3. Corporations, Nonprofit—Accounting—
Standards—United States. I. Title.
    HF5616.U5A599 1989
    657'.0218—dc19   88-30494
                                                       CIP

Contents

Preface

In 1978, the Financial Accounting Standards Board published my Research Report, *Financial Accounting in Nonbusiness Organizations: An Exploratory Study of Conceptual Issues.* Shortly thereafter, the FASB accepted responsibility for developing nonbusiness accounting standards. At that time, there were in existence four American Institute of CPAs Audit Guides and a Statement of Position recommending standards for various nonbusiness "industries." An FASB staff study identified some 35 major inconsistencies in these five documents. It therefore seemed likely that the Board's first priority would be to issue standards that would resolve these inconsistencies. This did not happen.

Instead, in 1979 the FASB designated these five statements, inconsistencies and all, as "preferable accounting principles." Until 1987, its only published documents on nonbusiness accounting were two Concepts Statements, Statement No. 4 on Objectives and Statement No. 6 on Elements of Financial Statements. In 1987, the FASB issued its first standard on nonbusiness accounting, Statement No. 93 on Depreciation. Most members of the nonbusiness task force, including me, found all these documents deficient. Over the past several years, I have pointed out their deficiencies in letters and memoranda totaling dozens of pages as well as in discussions with FASB staff. These comments apparently have had no impact. Part of the explanation may be that these materials generally focused on specific topics.

Consequently, I decided to write an overall analysis, giving my reasoning in some depth. This monograph is the result. A summary begins on page 1.

Acknowledgments

Professor Patricia Douglas, University of Montana, and Professor Wanda A. Wallace, Texas A&M University, made unusually thorough and perceptive comments on the manuscript.

I also appreciate the comments and suggestions of Freda S. Ackerman, Moody's Investors Service; Ronald J. Bossio, Financial Accounting Standards Board; Charles J. Christenson, Harvard Business School; F.A. Falk, Touche Ross & Co.; Robert T. Forrester, Coopers & Lybrand; Robert E. Field, Dartmouth College; James M. Fremgen, Naval Postgraduate School; T. Jack Gary, Jr.; Emerson O. Henke, Baylor University; David Hitchcock, Standard & Poor's Corporation; Gerald J. Holtz, Arthur Andersen & Co.; Delmer P. Hylton, Wake Forest University; Martin Ives, Governmental Accounting Standards Board; David Lyons, Rockefeller University; Paul Pacter, City of Stamford; Douglas E. Reinhardt, Colby College; William Rotch, University of Virginia; Keven Stevenson, Australian Accounting Research Foundation; John E. Stewart, Arthur Andersen & Co.; Earl R. Wilson, University of Missouri-Columbia; Venita Wood, Governmental Accounting Standards Board; W.T. Wrege, Ball State University; and David W. Young, Boston University.

I am grateful for the research and editorial assistance of my secretary, Judy Grady; Louis Bisgay, National Association of Accountants; Janet Daniels, University of Hartford; Mary Larkin, Miller Accounting Publications; Connie Rodriques, Harvard Business School, Garry Saletta, National Association of Accountants; and Lorna Daniels, Michele Marram, and Jeanne Walsh, Baker Library of Harvard Business School.

The views expressed herein are my own and not necessarily those of the persons named above.

Robert N. Anthony

Waterville Valley, New Hampshire
October 1988

Summary

1. INTRODUCTION

My answer to the question posed in the title of this monograph is, yes, nonbusiness accounting should be different from business accounting because nonbusiness accounting receives capital from contributors rather than from equity investors. However, this is the only significant difference. In all other respects, and especially in the measurement of net income, nonbusiness accounting standards should be the same as those applicable to business. I shall expand on this conclusion by supporting the following propositions:

1. Accounting standards for operating transactions should be the same in nonbusiness organizations as in business organizations.
2. Unlike most businesses, nonbusiness organizations receive equity capital from contributors. These contributions should be accounted for as capital inflows; they should not affect the measurement of income.
3. Nonbusiness organizations need separate funds to segregate operating transactions from contributed capital transactions. In other respects, the needs for separate

1

funds are the same in both business and nonbusiness organizations.

Background. Until the 1930s, business accounting and nonbusiness accounting were similar. Since then, the focus of business accounting has shifted from the balance sheet to the measurement of income. So did the focus of accounting in hospitals and in some other non-business industries. But government accounting and college and university accounting remained essentially unchanged. Some 35 inconsistencies exist among the standards that are applicable to various nonbusiness industries.

In 1978, the Financial Accounting Standards Board accepted responsibility for developing nonbusiness accounting standards. Its first such standard, Statement No. 93 on Depreciation, was published in 1987, nine years later.

Alleged Differences. The Financial Accounting Standards Board, the Governmental Accounting Standards Board, and others have listed many differences between business and nonbusiness organizations as reasons why the principles of business accounting are not applicable to nonbusiness organizations. With one exception, these differences relate to factors that have no effect on accounting (such as the absence of a profit motive in a nonbusiness organization), or objectives that financial accounting cannot accomplish (such as measuring service accomplishments in monetary terms), or objectives that accounting should not accomplish (such as comparing actual and budgeted performance, which would destroy the comparability of financial statements among organizations with different mandated budget formats). The fact that nonbusiness organizations do not have shareholders is not a relevant difference; it only means that nonbusiness accountants are not concerned with transactions involving shareholder equity.

The sole reason why business accounting principles are not entirely applicable to accounting in nonbusiness organizations is that nonbusiness organizations receive equity capital from contributors. Because this type of capital inflow has no counterpart in business, business accounting principles do not provide guidance.

2. INCOME MEASUREMENT

The primary focus of accounting in both business and nonbusiness organizations is on the measurement of net income so as to report the organization's success in maintaining its financial capital during an accounting period. Net income is broadly defined to include the effect of almost all changes in an organization's equity that are associated with events that happened in, or were discovered in, a given accounting period, other than changes in equity arising from flows of capital to and from external parties. Increases in equity (including gains) are revenues, and decreases (including losses) are expenses.

Standards for the measurement of net income should be the same in nonbusiness organizations as in businesses. However, the significance of the reported amount of net income—the bottom line on the operating statement—differs. In a business organization, as a general rule, the larger the net income, the better the financial performance. The financial performance of a nonbusiness organization was satisfactory if its net income was slightly greater than zero. A large net income indicates that the organization did not provide the services that it could have provided with available resources. In both types of organizations, net income reports whether the organization was financially viable, and in both types a persistent net loss leads ultimately to bankruptcy.

The GASB's concept of income is consistent with that described above. It uses the descriptive term "maintenance of interperiod equity" rather than "maintenance of financial capital."

In its Concepts Statement No. 6, the FASB adopted a different, and unsatisfactory, concept of the measurement of financial performance in nonbusiness organizations. The FASB labeled its concept, "changes in net assets." It includes both the results of operations during the period and also the inflows of equity capital from contributors. Capital contributions are unrelated to operating performance during the period. For example, reporting the receipt of endowment as an item of revenue on an operating statement would seriously distort the report of performance. The principal of an endowment (as distinguished from earnings on the endowment) cannot be used to finance the expenses of the current period, or indeed of any period.

The income-measurement concept accepted by most authorities other than the FASB suggests principles that should govern accounting for certain types of transactions in nonbusiness organizations. They are applicable to all nonbusiness industries.

Depreciation expense should be reported for all depreciable assets acquired with operating resources (either currently available funds or borrowed funds). Other possible reasons for recording depreciation have been stated, but I defer discussion of them to Part 3 in connection with the discussion of contributed capital assets. The need to report depreciation on depreciable assets assets acquired with operating resources in order to measure net income properly is a sufficient reason for depreciating these assets.

Accountants disagree about the amount of investment earnings to be recognized as revenue. Until recently, revenue was limited to dividends, interest, and similar income. Many organizations have now shifted to a "total-return/spending-rate concept." Until there is a consensus, the standard on this topic probably should permit either approach. The FASB approach is not consistent with either of these alternatives; it is flawed.

Pledges applicable to the operations of the current period should be recorded as revenues of the period. If the pledge is not paid by the end of the period, the amount should be carried as a receivable, with an appropriate adjustment for uncollectible accounts. Pledges applicable to future periods and pledges for capital contributions should not be recorded in the accounts. These amounts are soft estimates, and there is no need to book them in order to measure a period's net income.

Contributions for operating activities that will take place in future periods should be recorded as liabilities when they are received. They become revenues in the period in which expenses are incurred for these activities.

Although existing pronouncements on how to measure income in nonbusiness industries differ significantly, the differences reflect differences in the judgments of individual members of standards-setting bodies rather than inherent differences in the nature of accounting transactions.

The GASB's present plans would make government accounting consistent with business accounting, except for the treatment of depreciation; the GASB's rationale for a special treatment of depreciation is weak. The FASB seems to have gone out of its way to state differences that do not in fact exist.

3. CONTRIBUTED CAPITAL

Arriving at the proper distinction between income and capital (i.e., between operating flows and capital flows) is, and always has been, another central issue in accounting. Although the FASB recognizes that there is such a distinction (in ¶49 of Concepts Statement No. 4), this distinction has had no influence on FASB conclusions about concepts and standards.

Business enterprises obtain equity capital from two sources: (1) operating activities, which is an internal source reported on the balance sheet as retained earnings; and (2) equity investors, which is an external source, reported on the balance sheet as paid-in capital. Nonbusiness organizations also obtain equity capital from two sources: (1) operating activities, the same internal source as in business (for which "operating equity" is a better term than "retained earnings" on the balance sheet), and (2) capital contributions, which is an external source.

Capital contributions include plant and endowment received as a result of a capital campaign, bequests, legislative capital appropriations, and grants and contracts that provide capital assets. In all important respects, capital contributions are of the same nature as additions to paid-in capital. Both make the organization better off. Both are obtained at a cost. Both are external sources unrelated to the organization's operations. The FASB claims that there is a difference in that paid-in capital

5

represents a claim of the owners, whereas contributors have no corresponding claim. Actually, the amount of the owners' claim in a going concern has no relevance, and the amount received by shareholders in liquidation would be unrelated to the book amount of shareholders' equity, except by coincidence.

Changes in equity capital involving transactions with external sources never affect the measurement of income. Issuance of additional stock does not increase income, nor do dividends decrease income. The essential similarity between paid-in capital in a business and contributed capital in a nonbusiness organization requires that changes in contributed capital should never affect the measurement of income.

The GASB agrees with this conclusion. The FASB does not. Instead of distinguishing between operating contributions and capital contributions, the FASB divides resource inflows into three "classes": unrestricted, temporarily restricted, and permanently restricted. This three-way classification does not correspond to that in any existing accounting framework, and it is inconsistent with the basic distinction between operating flows and capital flows.

The FASB's approach requires that contributions of plant be classified in the same way as contributions to the annual alumni fund. It requires that assets contributed to endowment be included with operating assets, even though these assets legally cannot be used for operating purposes.

In Statement No. 93, the FASB required that depreciation on contributed plant be reported as an expense. This treatment is illogical. The rationale cannot be that such depreciation is relevant in measuring net income because this depreciation relates to contributed capital, and capital transactions with external parties should not affect the measurement of income. Unless there are other benefits of reporting it, depreciation on contributed plant should not be reported at all.

Few of the asserted reasons for reporting such depreciation are valid, and those that are valid do not apply to most organizations. If worthwhile benefits can be demonstrated, this depreciation can be reported as an expense with an exactly equal amount reported as revenue in the same period, so that there is no effect on net income. This is the approach recommended in International Accounting Standard No. 20. At most, reporting depreciation on contributed plant should be optional, at the organization's discretion.

4. FINANCIAL STATEMENTS

Both business and nonbusiness organizations have funds: pension funds, trust funds, agency funds. These are necessary in order to separate the organization's own assets from those for which it is acting as trustee or agent. Government organizations have several unnecessary funds as well as two "account groups" that are single-entry listings masquerading as components of a double-entry system. Most are holdovers from the traditional focus on current assets and current liabilities. They permit manipulation, and they make the financial statements difficult to understand.

There is only one special requirement for funds in nonbusiness organizations. Funds are necessary to separate information about the status and flow of contributed capital from information about the status and flow of operating items. Some organizations may prefer to use other funds for internal control purposes; they should be permitted to do so. The financial statements that report on operating activities should consist of a balance sheet, an operating statement, and a cash flow statement. There should be supplemental reports on segments of the organization, such as the separate governmental and business-type activities of a municipality.

The financial statements for contributed capital should consist of a balance sheet (or a separate section of an overall balance sheet) and a statement of increases and decreases of contributed capital. The latter resembles the business statement of increases and decreases in equity capital.

5. IMPLICATIONS

My analysis suggests that the Financial Accounting Standards Board should issue a standard dealing with the accounting problems in nonprofit organizations; should modify Statement No. 93 to require depreciation only on operating assets; and should either amend Concepts Statements No. 4 and No. 6 or refrain from using them as a guide in developing nonbusiness standards. The AICPA should revise its nonbusiness Audit Guides to make them consistent with generally accepted accounting principles, or it should permit industry associations to develop their own accounting guides. The GASB should issue a standard similar to its Exposure Draft on measurement focus.

Accounting standards are man-made. If more than one standards-setting body exists, differences in individual judgments will lead to inconsistent standards for the same transactions. Therefore, standards-setting bodies for colleges and universities, or for nonprofit organizations as a whole, should not be created. The GASB should complete its mission in the next few years and then go out of existence. It should be replaced by a permanent task force that will play an important role in the development of accounting standards that affect government organizations.

The changes suggested here will lead to the elimination of the detail that makes for complicated fund-accounting courses requiring much rote memory. The additional course time thus made available can be used for material on the management uses of accounting information, either in service organizations generally and/or in health care and other specific service industries.

1

Introduction

Dartmouth-Hitchcock Medical Center consists of several separate legal entities: the Center itself, which is a management and coordinating body; a hospital; a physician's clinic; and a medical school. In its general-purpose financial statements, the Medical Center follows American Institute of Certified Public Accountants (AICPA) Statement of Position 78-10 for "other nonprofit organizations"; the hospital follows the AICPA Audit Guide for Hospitals; the clinic uses business accounting; and the medical school follows the AICPA Audit Guide for Colleges and Universities.

The accounting principles specified by these four sources are so different that consolidated financial statements for the Medical Center cannot be prepared. The Medical Center trustees receive separate financial statements for each entity. As an accountant with experience in each of these types of organizations, I think I understand these statements. Nonaccountants do not. Some of my fellow trustees chide me about this muddled state of affairs. They ask, Can't you accountants straighten out this mess?

And there is indeed a mess. Nonbusiness organizations use financial accounting principles that are different for various nonbusiness industries and different from business accounting principles. In fact, a Financial Accounting Standards Board (FASB) staff memorandum of March 11, 1981, listed 35 major differences. The schism between business and nonbusiness accounting is manifest in many ways. There is a government and nonprofit section of the American Accounting Association (AAA). Colleges and universities offer hundreds of courses on government and nonprofit accounting; these courses focus on the brand of accounting called "fund accounting," which is regarded as a separate subject. Government accountants have their own professional association, their own journal, and even their own Governmental Accounting Standards Board (GASB).

By contrast, the general-purpose financial statements of business corporations are prepared in accordance with a single set of accounting principles—even though accountants in financial institutions, manufacturing companies, mining companies, merchandising companies, and service companies encounter vastly different types of transactions. They have no AAA section. There are few professional journals, and only a few universities offer industry-specific courses.[1] Although there are Audit Guides and Accounting Guides for certain industries, these are (or at least are supposed to be) consistent with the single set of business accounting standards.

The issues that nonprofit trustees discuss are similar to those that corporate directors discuss: share of market, pricing policy, market segmentation, competitive strategies, compensation, pensions, other fringe benefits, productivity, quality control, and so on. Like corporate directors, nonbusiness trustees spend much time analyzing the financial results of operations. Nevertheless, nonbusiness accounting is different from business accounting, and some of the differences are alleged to reflect fundamental differences in accounting requirements.

PROPOSITIONS

Why is nonbusiness accounting so different? I believe that, with one exception, the answer lies in tradition, rather than in any inherent difference between business and nonbusiness accounting transactions. The exception results from a difference in the source of capital in the two types of organizations. Specifically, I shall support the following propositions:

1. Accounting standards for operating transactions should be the same in nonbusiness organizations as in business organizations.

2. Unlike most businesses, nonbusiness organizations receive equity capital from contributors. These contributions should be accounted for as capital inflows; they should not affect the measurement of income.

3. Nonbusiness organizations need separate funds to segregate operating transactions from contributed capital transactions. In other respects, the needs for separate funds are the same in both business and nonbusiness organizations.

I shall discuss the implications of these propositions on FASB Statement No. 93 (on depreciation in nonprofit organizations), FASB Concepts Statements No. 4 and No. 6, other FASB pronouncements on nonprofit accounting, AICPA Audit Guides, and GASB standards. There are also important implications for academic courses in government and nonprofit accounting.

These propositions are closely related. I discuss them separately because this is the clearest way of making my point.

BACKGROUND

Business and Nonbusiness Organizations

Nonbusiness organizations are legally distinguished from businesses in two ways. First, their goal is something other than earning a profit; essentially, the goal is to provide services. Second, they do not receive capital from equity investors and hence do not pay dividends. There are approximately 1.2 million nonbusiness organizationsin the United States, and they employ about 25 percent of the nonagricultural work force.[2]

Nonbusiness organizations are usually divided into two categories: government and nonprofit.[3] I shall argue that the accounting principles are the same for both classes.

I do not discuss federal government accounting, which is different in important respects from other non-business accounting.[4] Because the federal government can print money, its accounting is not governed by the need to measure the extent to which it has maintained its financial capital, which is an important objective of both business and nonbusiness accounting.

Development of Business Accounting

Until World War I, financial accounting principles in the United States were derived from textbooks, regulatory bodies, and trade associations. Textbook authors based their writings on their personal perceptions of good practice. Regulatory bodies prescribed accounting principles for the companies they regulated. The influence of trade associations resulted in similar practices for companies in certain industries. But there were no overall authoritative standards.

The emphasis of accounting was on "accountability" in the narrow sense of reporting how well management safeguarded the organization's assets. For this reason and also because most funds were obtained from bankers who were interested in liquidity, the focus was on the balance sheet, especially current assets and current liabilities. Although accounting principles were established in England by law in 1844, British law did not require an income statement until 1928 [Chatfield 1977, p. 118].

In the United States, financial statements were generally on a cash or an expenditure basis, rather than on an expense basis. Depreciation was not widely recognized in the accounts until after the passage of the Revenue Act of 1913, which permitted depreciation as a tax-deductible item [Hendriksen 1982, pp. 30, 31].

In the 1920s and 1930s, the number of public stock offerings rose sharply, and equity investors demanded financial statements that reported performance. Accordingly, accounting rapidly shifted from a focus on the balance sheet to a focus on the income statement and the measurement of net income.[5] The going concern, accrual, and matching concepts were emphasized. The expense basis superseded the cash or expenditure basis [Hendriksen 1982, pp. 29–36].

The American Institute of CPAs began to issue material on accounting in 1917, initially in cooperation with the Federal Reserve Board. Most of its statements related to auditing rather than to accounting principles. Although the Securities Act of 1933 and the Securities and Exchange Act of 1934 authorized the Securities and Exchange Commission (SEC) to prescribe accounting standards, the SEC decided to permit the AICPA to continue to take the lead. In 1938, the AICPA established a Committee on Accounting Procedure as a standards-setting body. It issued "Opinions," not "Standards"; however, accountants knew that the Securities and Exchange Commission expected these opinions to be followed [Chatfield 1977, Ch. 9].

The current standards-setting body is the Financial Accounting Standard Board, which was established in 1973. It issues standards, and these are "generally accepted accounting principles," defined as such by Rule 203 of the AICPA. Except in highly unusual circumstances, an entity's auditors must give a qualified opinion on financial statements that do not conform to these standards. The FASB has also issued six concepts statements. These are intended to provide a conceptual foundation for its own deliberations. They do not constitute generally accepted accounting principles, however; preparers of financial statements are not required to follow them.

Development of Nonbusiness Accounting

Nonbusiness accounting also dates from the nineteenth century. In the early years, good practice was described in textbooks and in manuals prepared for various nonbusiness industries.[6] I shall discuss government accounting separately from nonprofit accounting because its history is somewhat different.

Government Accounting. In the early decades of the twentieth century, state and municipal accounting was influenced by legislative statutes. By 1920, 44 states had laws that specified how budgets were to be prepared [Chatfield 1977, p. 193], and accountants naturally followed these statutes. These budgets were on either a cash basis, an encumbrance basis, or a mixture of these two bases.[7]

As a consequence of fiscal crises during the depression years, the National Committee on Municipal Accounting was created in 1934; its first statement, *Principles of Municipal Accounting,* was issued in the same year. The members of the National Committee and its successor organizations were unpaid volunteers, supported by a small professional staff (initially, one person). These organizations issued several revisions to the initial statement, the last being in 1979.[8] Because its principles conflicted with statutes enacted by many state legislatures, only a few municipalities followed them until recently. (By constitutional law, municipalities are subordinate to their states.)

Although in the 1930s the focus of business accounting shifted from the balance sheet to an emphasis on performance as reported on the income statement, government accounting continued to focus on accountability for assets, as reported on the balance sheet, specifically on current assets and current liabilities. This focus perpetuated the traditional British practice of the "double balance sheet," with one section for current items and the other for noncurrent items, a practice that was commonly seen in both business and nonbusiness accounting until the 1930s. Also, the outflows were measured in terms of expenditures rather than expenses.[9]

The National Committee perpetuated the focus on current items. For example, although its system was described as "fund accounting," fixed assets and noncurrent liabilities were not recorded in any fund; rather, they were listed in "groups of accounts," which were essentially single-entry records, not tied to the fund system; this practice continues today. Many state laws shifted away from the cash or encumbrance basis to that prescribed by the municipal standards-setting agency.

In the 1970s, Cleveland defaulted on its bonds (a rare occurrence), and New York, Chicago, Detroit, and several other large cities almost went bankrupt. Their accounting systems were widely criticized because the financial statements did not reveal the serious financial situation.

Consequently, there was strong public sentiment for better accounting standards. Initially, the thought was that the FASB would assume responsibility for setting these standards, but municipal accounting organizations strongly resisted yielding jurisdiction to the FASB. After several years of discussion, the Governmental Accounting Standards Board was created in 1984. For the first time, there was a governmental standards-setting body with a prestigious Board and a sizable staff.

In December 1987, the Governmental Accounting Standards Board issued an Exposure Draft, *Measurement Focus and Basis of Accounting—Governmental Funds.* If adopted, it will make the measurement focus for government accounting consistent with that for business accounting, except that it will continue a sort-of expenditure basis for fixed assets, rather than requiring that they be depreciated, and it will permit (but not require) the expenditure basis for inventory items.

Nonprofit Accounting. Until the 1960s, individual nonprofit industry associations developed accounting guidance for their members.[10] For example, an accounting guide for YMCAs was published in 1919 and revised several times thereafter. In the 1950s, a strong movement developed to arrive at principles that were generally applicable to nonprofit organizations. Its impetus came partly from foundations and other contributors and partly from certified public accountants. The latter were required to state whether the financial statements they audited were "in conformance with generally accepted accounting principles," but there was no authoritative statement describing these principles for nonprofit organizations.

In the absence of a central coordinating body, several nonbusiness industry associations developed accounting principles for their members. In the 1970s, some of these were published as AICPA Audit Guides or Statements of Position. In the following paragraphs, I will describe briefly the history of these documents.

In 1954, the National Health Council and the National Social Welfare Assembly, umbrella organizations for 54 philanthropic organizations, published *Standards of Accounting and Financial Reporting for Voluntary Health and*

Welfare Organizations. It recommended a fund-accounting system, with many aspects of accrual accounting, but depreciation was made optional. (In later revisions, depreciation was required.) The AICPA adopted most of the principles in this document in its Audit Guide for Voluntary Health and Welfare Organizations, which was most recently revised in 1974.

College and university accounting was codified in 1910, seven years before the first official pronouncement for business accounting.[11] Its most important revision was made in the 1950s by a committee chaired by Lloyd Morey, president of the University of Illinois. Morey had written a text on government accounting, in which he maintained that reporting depreciation in government organizations was worthless. The ideas contained in that text influenced the college and university publication. Morey was also vice chairman of the National Committee on Municipal Accounting, which probably explains why both college accounting and municipal accounting have the only two sets of principles that do not require depreciation, or at least recommend it, and that carry fund accounting to extremes.

The AICPA Audit Guide for Colleges and Universities was issued in 1975. It does not require an operating statement. Indeed, it says [pp. 55–56] that the closest financial statement to an operating statement "does not purport to present the results of operations or the net income or loss for the period"; this is an important objective of most financial accounting systems.

Hospital accounting has been similar to business accounting for many years. Although the Hospital Audit Guide is usually included in lists of nonprofit accounting pronouncements, the guide itself states that it is applicable to hospitals of all types: governmental, voluntary (i.e., nonprofit), and proprietary (i.e., for-profit). The AICPA Hospital Audit Guide was issued in 1972.

In 1978, the AICPA issued Statement of Position 78-10, "Accounting Principles and Reporting Practices for Certain Nonprofit Organizations." It was intended to apply to all nonprofit organizations not covered by other Audit Guides, but the dividing line is not clear. For example, some private preparatory schools and junior colleges follow the College and University Audit Guide, but most use Statement of Position 78-10.

In 1979, the FASB designated these statements as "preferable accounting principles." This means that if an entity changes its accounting practice, the change must be in the direction of the applicable Audit Guide or Statement of Position [FAS 32].

As noted earlier, these Audit Guides and Statement of Position 78-10 differ from one another in 35 major ways. They even differ in the treatment of certain transactions that are identical in all nonbusiness organizations, for example, the measurement of endowment revenue. College and university accounting is basically different from business accounting. Government accounting currently is also different, but it is moving rapidly toward business accounting. Other nonprofit organizations have accounting principles that are similar to business accounting in most respects; however, they are sufficiently different so that the accountant (and student) cannot rely on business accounting principles in deciding how to record a transaction. These differences reflect individual preferences of the committees that wrote them (or of a persuasive committee member) rather than differences in the information needs of those who use the financial statements.

Overall Standards. Until 1978, the AICPA Committee on Accounting Procedures and successor standards-setting bodies focused most of their efforts on issues that affected businesses. Accounting Research Bulletin No. 43, which restated the preceding bulletins, contained the following:

> The committee has not directed its attention to accounting problems or procedures of religious, charitable, scientific, educational, and similar non-profit institutions, municipalities, professional firms, and the like. Accordingly, except where there is a specific statement of a different intent by the committee, its opinions and recommendations are directed primarily to business enterprises organized for profit [ARB 43, Introduction, ¶5].

The Financial Accounting Standards Board, established in 1973, continued to focus its attention on accounting issues that were important for businesses, although its standards were made applicable to nonbusiness organizations if the topic was relevant to them. Of its six concepts statements, No. 1, No. 2, No. 3, and No. 5 were initially limited to business enterprises.

In 1978, the FASB added the topic of nonbusiness organizations to its agenda; in 1980, it published Concepts Statement No. 4, *Objectives of Financial Reporting by Nonbusiness Organizations;* and in 1985, it published Concepts Statement No. 6, which made Concepts Statement No. 2 on *Qualitative Characteristics of Accounting Information* applicable to nonprofits and expanded Concepts Statement No. 3 on *Elements of Financial Statements of Business Enterprises* to include elements for nonprofit organizations. Its first standard dealing with a nonbusiness problem was Statement No. 93, *Recognition of Depreciation by Not-for-Profit Organizations,* published in August 1987, almost 10 years after nonbusiness accounting was added to its agenda. There was strong opposition to this standard; consequently, its effective date was deferred to 1990. It therefore is in limbo as of the date of this monograph.

Definition of the Entity

None of the standards or concepts statements of the FASB and the GASB has addressed the issue of defining the nonbusiness entity. In a business, the consolidated entity is defined in terms of the percentage ownership of common or voting stock, but because nonbusiness organizations do not have common stock, the relation between the "parent" and its affiliated bodies requires other criteria. The National Council on Governmental Accounting, predecessor of the GASB, made an attempt to describe criteria in its Statement No. 3, but there is general agreement that this statement is inadequate. Studies have been made or are underway in both nonprofit and government organizations.[12] The entity definition topic is omitted from this monograph. It does not affect accounting standards for the consolidated entity, except those relating to the relationship between the parent and its affiliated units.

Summary

Until the 1930s, business accounting and nonbusiness accounting were similar. Thereafter, business accounting made progress. So did accounting in hospitals and certain other types of nonbusiness organizations. But government accounting and college and university accounting remained essentially unchanged. Part of the explanation is the personal opinions of those involved in the standards-setting process. As a result, similar transactions are recorded inconsistently by nonbusiness organizations of various types and by business and nonbusiness organizations.

ALLEGED DIFFERENCES

In this section, I discuss certain alleged differences between business and nonbusiness organizations. I will show that only one of these differences—the fact that nonbusiness organizations receive contributed capital—is a valid reason for requiring different accounting concepts or standards for nonbusiness organizations.

Financial Accounting Standards Board Analysis

FASB Concepts Statement No. 4 [¶6] lists three "major distinguishing characteristics" of a nonbusiness entity. Except for the presence of contributed capital, none is a valid reason for requiring different accounting concepts or standards.

The first is, "Receipts of significant amounts of resources from resource providers who do not expect to receive either repayment or economic benefits proportionate to resources provided." These resource receipts may be either capital contributions or operating contributions. The fact that nonbusiness organizations have capital contributions is indeed a distinguishing characteristic. The central thesis of this monograph, discussed in depth in Part 3, is that these contributions rarely occur in business organizations, that existing standards do not deal with them, and that failure to discuss capital contributions explicitly is the principal defect of existing FASB standards.

Contributions related to operating activities are another matter. These contributions fit the definition of revenue in FASB Concepts Statement No. 6 [CON 6 ¶78]: "Revenues are inflows . . . during a period from delivering or producing goods, rendering services, or *other activities that constitute the entity's major or central operations*" [emphasis added]. Try convincing a college president that obtaining annual contributions to the alumni fund is not a "major or central operation." A dollar of alumni fund contributions pays bills just as does a dollar of tuition. The difference between the amount of these contributions and the cost of obtaining them is a "gross margin," similar to the difference between sales revenue and cost of sales in a business. Indeed, ¶113 of Concepts Statement No. 6 specifically classifies most fund-raising activities as "ongoing major activities that constitute the organization's central operations . . ." If one were to quibble on this point, there can be no doubt that operating contributions are at least "gains" which are defined as: "increases in equity . . . from all other transactions affecting the entity except those that result from revenues and investments by owners" [CON 6 ¶82]. Both revenues and gains are increases in income.

The second of FASB's distinguishing characteristics is, "Operating purposes that are other than to provide goods or services at a profit or profit equivalent." This is simply the legal distinction between a for-profit and a nonprofit organization. The FASB does not indicate what difference this makes in accounting in the two types of organizations—specifically in the measurement of revenues or expenses for the purpose of reporting whether the entity has maintained its financial capital. Regardless of an organization's purpose, it has maintained its financial capital if its revenues (including gains) at least equal its expenses (including losses).

The third characteristic is, "Absence of defined ownership interests that can be sold, transferred, or redeemed, or that convey entitlement to a share of a residual distribution of resources in the event of liquidation of the organization." Again, this simply defines a nonprofit organization. Although the absence of ownership interests complicates the problem of defining the accounting entity, it has nothing to do with the measurement of income. Since transactions with owners do not exist in a nonbusiness organization, the nonbusiness accountant isn't concerned with them.

After listing these characteristics, paragraph 6 of Concepts Statement No. 4 concludes with the following:

> These characteristics result in certain types of transactions that are largely, although not entirely, absent in business enterprises, such as contributions and grants, and to the absence of transactions with owners, such as issuing and redeeming stock and paying dividends.

The implication that this is a reason for differences in business and nonbusiness accounting is a fallacy. The absence of a transaction in either type of organization does not mean that there is a *difference* in treatment. It means only that if a certain type of transaction doesn't occur, the entity doesn't have to deal with it. Some companies don't have capital leases; others don't have convertible bonds. The only effect on accounting entries is that these companies don't have to worry about the treatment of these items. *A valid difference in treatment results only when the objectives of financial reporting require that a business entity treat a transaction in one way and a nonbusiness entity treat the same transaction in a different way.*

Governmental Accounting Standards Board Analysis

In its Statement No. 1, the GASB listed and discussed eight "characteristics of the governmental environment that affect financial reporting":

a. Primary characteristics of government's structure and the services it provides:
(1) The representative form of government and the separation of powers
(2) The federal system of government and the prevalence of intergovernmental revenues
(3) The relationship of taxpayers to services received

21

b. Control characteristics resulting from government's structure:
(1) The budget as an expression of public policy and financial intent and as a method of providing control
(2) The use of fund accounting for control purposes
c. Other characteristics:
(1) The dissimilarities between similarly designated governments
(2) The significant investment in non-revenue-producing capital assets
(3) The nature of the political process. [GASB CS. 1, ¶12–¶29]

Nevertheless, "The Board has concluded that there are no major differences in the financial reporting objectives of governmental-type and business-type activities" [¶75].

In ¶77–¶79 of its Statement No. 1, the GASB listed nine objectives of government reporting, taking into account the differences listed earlier. Six of these objectives are the same as those that are relevant for business financial statements; therefore, they are not factors that lead to differences in accounting. These are listed and the reasons why they do not lead to differences in accounting are mentioned:

- "Measuring interperiod equity" is the same as measuring the maintenance of financial capital, as will be discussed in the next Part.
- "Information about the sources and uses of financial resources" is provided by the cash flow statement and related schedules.
- "Information about how the governmental entity financed its activities and met its cash requirements" is also provided by the cash flow statement.
- "Information about whether the entity's financial position improved or deteriorated" is provided by comparative balance sheets.
- "Information about the financial position and condition of a governmental entity" is provided by the balance sheet.

- "Legal or contractual restrictions on resources and risks of potential loss of resources" are disclosed by the balance sheet and accompanying notes.

Two of the three remaining objectives cannot feasibly be accomplished by any financial reporting system. The third is feasible, but it would inhibit the comparability of accounting reports.

The first of these other three objectives is that accounting should "assess the service potential of [long-lived resources]." Accounting cannot do this. The net book value of depreciable assets does not purport to measure remaining service potential; the number reports only that portion of original cost that has not yet been charged as an operating expense. To report "remaining service potential" would require annual estimates by expert engineers or appraisers. Few people would assert that the cost of making these appraisals would be worthwhile. If information on service potential were to be reported, it would have to be as supplementary information, not as part of the financial statements.

The second objective is that accounting should provide information about service efforts and accomplishments. Accounting can provide information about the costs of providing services, which is a measure of "effort"; however, in most nonbusiness organizations, accounting cannot provide information about "accomplishments." In a business, net income is a measure of "accomplishment" because profitability is an important business objective.[13] Basically, the objective of a nonbusiness entity is to provide service. The *cost* of providing services can be reported, but reporting the *value* of these services, or even the quantity or quality of the services rendered, is beyond the capability of financial accounting. Both the GASB and the FASB have commissioned studies on this topic. None of the resulting reports has found that measuring the value of services in monetary amounts would be feasible.[14]

Annual reports should indeed provide information about the quantity and quality of the services that the organization has provided, but this information is necessarily included as a supplement to the basic financial statements. Most of it is nonfinancial, that is, it is not obtained from the debit-and-credit accounting system. Furthermore, the nature of this information varies so much among different types of organizations that a relevant standard would necessarily be vague. For example, the United Way of America describes 587 programs that are carried out by United Way agencies and lists one or more performance measures for each of them in a 250-page book.[15] For both these reasons, a standard issued by a financial accounting standards body would not be feasible or useful. This is a job for industry associations.

The third objective—demonstrating compliance with the budget—can be reported, but a standards-setting body should not require that general-purpose financial statements be consistent with the organization's budget. Budgets for many government organizations are prepared according to rules prescribed in state or other statutes, and these requirements vary widely. Thus, the numbers in an accounting report that is prepared in a prescribed budget format and with prescribed definitions cannot be compared with the numbers in reports that are prepared by organizations using different formats and definitions. Comparability is an essential requirement of accounting reports [CON 2 ¶111–¶119 and GASB Cod Sec. 100.168].

If the legislature required that budgets be prepared in accordance with generally accepted accounting principles, this comparability might be achieved. Some states already have such a requirement, and others are considering it. If all states eventually adopt these principles, a standard will be unnecessary. Until all of them do so, a standard is unworkable because the GASB cannot require legislatures to adhere to its standards.

Moreover, budgets are often revised during the year, sometimes for good reasons, but other times simply to make the budget match the actuals. Comparing actuals with a budget revised for the latter reason is meaningless. Developing criteria for deciding on valid reasons for revising a budget is difficult but not impossible.

However, no financial accounting standards body has attempted to develop such criteria, as far as I know.

The main point is that the objectives of government accounting are essentially the same as those for business accounting. In fact, the proposal in the GASB Measurement Focus Exposure Draft contains only one significant difference from business accounting; that one relates to depreciation. The relevance of this difference will be examined in a later section.

Other Alleged Differences

Many articles and many letters to the FASB and the GASB have the same theme: "Our organization is different." I list some of these alleged differences below and explain why none is a valid reason for having different accounting standards.

1. Nonprofits don't have a profit motive. Obviously, the operating statement of a nonprofit organization doesn't measure profitability. It does (or should) measure whether the organization has maintained its financial capital. As will be explained in Part 2, the principles involved in this measurement are exactly the same for business and nonbusiness organizations. The difference lies in the meaning of the "bottom line," not in how the bottom line is calculated.

2. Because nonprofits are service organizations, their financial statements should tell the "service story." As explained earlier, the basic financial statements for most nonbusiness organizations can't report the value, quantity, or quality of services provided. They can report the costs of various types of services, and the principles for doing this are the same in a nonbusiness organization as in business. Information about accomplishments is necessarily supplemental information, and most is nonfinancial, even nonmonetary, in nature. Moreover, information about accomplishments varies greatly with the type of organization. A standard prescribing such information would necessarily be so general as not to convey much substance. This is another task that should be left to industry associations.

3. A nonprofit should not use accrual accounting because it may not have the funds to pay its accrued costs. This argument is advanced with particular reference to pension expense. It indicates either a failure to understand the purpose of accounting or a deliberate attempt to misuse accounting by hiding the actual situation. Pension costs incurred for services rendered in the current period are truly expenses of that period, whether or not funds were available to pay for them. Failure to report these expenses in effect pushes part of the pension burden forward to future periods. If an organization has not earned sufficient revenues to provide for all its expenses of the current year, including its pension expense, it has not broken even. As will be explained later, this is the concept of "maintenance of financial capital" or "interperiod equity."

4. Users of financial statements have different needs. Several studies have identified users of financial statements prepared by nonbusiness organizations. Banks, other creditors, bond rating agencies, and third-party payers are included as users in most such lists, but the studies do not indicate how, if at all, the accounting principles governing the information needed to appraise the creditworthiness of a nonbusiness organization differ from those needed to make a similar appraisal of a business.[16] The studies also identify other users, but they do not explain what, if any, different accounting principles are needed to satisfy these needs. Those who make this argument should demonstrate how the needs of other users are sufficiently different from the needs of users of financial statements of businesses to justify different standards for nonbusiness organizations. I am not aware of any such demonstration. Taxpayers and citizen groups acting in their behalf often ask for simplified financial statements, but these are derived from the regular financial statements; they are not prepared according to different principles.

5. Recipients of services don't necessarily pay for them. This is so. Nevertheless, the amounts they do pay are revenues, and the amounts the organization receives to make up the difference between its service revenues and its expenses are also revenues.

6. There is no causal connection between revenues and expenses. For many transactions, this is true. However, even in a business, there is no causal connection between the revenues of a period and research/development costs, extraordinary losses, discontinued segments, and many components of general and administrative costs. The lack of a causal connection does not lead to a difference in accounting principles.

7. Nonprofits have "nonreciprocal transfers." This fancy phrase appeared first in APB Statement No. 4 [¶62]. It means "transfers in one direction of resources or obligations, either from the enterprise to other organizations or from other organizations to the enterprise." For businesses, nonreciprocal transfers are principally receipts from and payments to shareholders. For nonbusiness enterprises, nonreciprocal transfers consist of contributions, broadly defined. In Part 3, I shall show that certain types of contributions are revenues and should be treated the same as other items of revenues. In Part 4, I shall show that other types are capital contributions and should be treated the same as transfers from shareholders. In other words, the term "nonreciprocal transfer" is not a relevant distinction. Some nonreciprocal transfers affect the measurement of income; others do not.

8. Nonprofits don't pay income taxes. This fact is irrelevant. It means only that nonprofits don't have to deal with the intricacies of income-tax accounting. Even in a business, financial accounting is not governed by IRS regulations.

9. Nonprofits use general-purpose financial statements for internal management purposes. Indeed they do, but so do for-profit organizations. The use made of financial statements by trustees and management is essentially the same as the use made by outside parties, except that internal users study the numbers in more depth. In any event, the external general-purpose financial statements cannot be governed by the needs of internal users, and standards-setting bodies do not in fact prescribe standards for this purpose.

10. Government organizations are political. One of the implications of this statement is that elected officials tend to manipulate financial reports and that this tendency is less likely to be checked in a government organization; in a business, the audit committee of the board of directors may serve as such a check. It follows that there is a greater need for accounting standards in a government organization. Without debating the validity of this implication, it does not appear to lead to different accounting principles in government organizations.

Summary

With the exception of capital contributions, none of the alleged differences between business and nonbusiness organizations suggest that nonbusiness financial statements should be governed by different principles. Although alleged differences are cited by the FASB, the GASB, and others, none of these has merit.

2

Income Measurement

Primacy of Income Measurement

The most important objective of financial accounting is to measure the net income of a period and to report it on the income statement. In 1922, William A. Paton wrote:

> Net revenue [Paton's term for net income] is the first significant conclusion drawn by the accountant at the end of the accounting period.[17]

In 1938, Sanders, Hatfield, and Moore wrote:

> The division of the life of a business enterprise into fiscal periods has created the problem of determining the income of the enterprise for each fiscal period. This determination is a most important task of accounting.[18]

In 1943, George O. May wrote:

> The most important statement is that which discloses the amount and sources of income.[19]

In its first concepts statement, the FASB wrote:

> The primary focus of financial reporting is information about an enterprise's financial perfor-

mance provided by measures of earnings and its components [CON 1 ¶43].

The net income of a period is the amount reported in the press, the focus of analysts' review, and the amount that people have in mind when they judge how well a company has performed. Readers of financial statements look at the monetary items on the balance sheet, but they pay relatively little attention to the nonmonetary items, other than inventory.

A few people cling to the view that the purpose of accounting is to report on management's accountability for the assets entrusted to it, but the overwhelming majority would agree with the quotations from accounting greats given above: the most important task of the accountant is to measure the amount of net income and report it on the income statement. I belabor this obvious point because I shall say little about the balance sheet in the analysis that follows, and I trust that readers will not claim that the analysis is inadequate for this reason.

The Concept of Net Income

Until 1966, organizations had wide latitude in defining "net income," which is the bottom line of the income statement. In that year, the Accounting Principles Board issued Opinion No. 9, "Reporting the Results of Operations," which stated that net income should include the effect on equity of almost all transactions occurring in an accounting period, other than inflows of resources from equity investors (e.g., issuance of additional stock) and distributions to equity investors (e.g., dividends). Opinion No. 9 applied to all organizations, except that differences in format were permitted for financial institutions and certain [unspecified] nonprofit organizations [APB 9, ¶6]. APB Opinion No. 30 (1973) added transactions involving the disposal of a business segment and extraordinary gains and losses as items affecting net income. Many FASB standards state how specific types of transactions should be treated in the measurement of income. Many of these standards apply to both business and nonbusiness organizations.

Conceptually, the *measurement* of net income is the same in both business and nonprofit organizations. Its essential characteristics are:

1. Net income relates to events that happened in a given accounting period or events that came to light in that period.

2. These events are revenues (including gains realized in the period) and expenses (including losses that occurred or were discovered in the period). Revenues and expenses are interpreted broadly to include most events that affect equity during the period, other than capital transactions. (A few highly unusual transactions, such as aspects of foreign exchange transactions, may be debited or credited directly to equity without flowing through the income statement.)[20]

3. Net income reports the amount of income that the entity *did* earn. It does not forecast what will happen in the future.

4. The amounts of revenues and expenses are, with a few exceptions, actual monetary amounts. After a five-year test of possibilities for adjusting historical-cost amounts for changes in the price level, the FASB decided not to require such a principle, even for supplementary information.[21]

5. Break-even financial performance means that revenues equal expenses. An organization has maintained its financial capital in an accounting period if it broke even in that period.

Accounting does not, and does not purport to, measure net income perfectly in either business or non-business organizations. Many items, such as bad debt expense and warranty expense and—above all—depreciation, are based on estimates of what will happen in the unknown future. Some actual losses may not come to light in the current period. Some expenditures that benefit future periods, such as research/development, are expensed because the measurement of future benefits is highly uncertain. Some FASB standards were adopted by a 4-to-3 vote, which indicates that a sizable minority did not agree. Statements No. 19 and No. 25 on Oil and

Gas Accounting, and Statement No. 71 on Regulatory Accounting, are examples.

The fact that the accounting model is imperfect is not a reason for rejecting it, however. As of now, it is the best that the profession can do, and we live with it. Its imperfections are irrelevant in examining the differences between business and nonbusiness accounting.

FASB Concept: Changes in Net Assets

The FASB concepts statements do not refer to "net income" in nonbusiness organizations. Concepts Statement No. 4 [¶67] does say that the types of information financial reporting can provide to help satisfy users' needs are similar in business and nonbusiness organizations, except for differences in terminology, and it makes a point-by-point comparison of these similarities.

Nevertheless, Concepts Statement No. 6 uses the idea of "changes in net assets" rather than "net income." "Net assets" is the arithmetic difference between total assets and total liabilities; "changes in net assets" are all such changes that occurred during the accounting period. These changes include the transactions that enter into the measurement of net income, as explained earlier, *plus* transactions that change the organization's capital. The latter are capital contributions. The result of combining these two types of transactions is an essentially meaningless, or even misleading, number.

A simple illustration can demonstrate its defects. Assume that in 1988 a certain college had revenues of $5 million, all from tuition, that it had expenses of $6 million, and that it received a bequest of $2 million that was its first contribution to endowment. The FASB would add the $2 million endowment contribution to the $5 million tuition revenue, making $7 million of "resource inflows," and would report a $1 million positive change in net assets. Such a report would imply that the college operated at a surplus, that its financial performance was good, and that it was financially viable.

If knowledgeable people were asked to comment on this situation, almost all of them would say that the college operated at a $1 million deficit; that its financial performance was poor; and that if it continued to operate in this fashion, it would not be viable (except in the unrealistic event that it would receive substantial endowments in the future).

The conceptual flaw in the FASB's approach is the failure to distinguish between operating activities and capital activities. It will be discussed in Part 3, which deals with contributed capital.

In Concepts Statement No. 6, the FASB divides changes in net assets into three classes. As will be shown in Part 3, this does not cure the problem because none of these classes approximates the concept of net income.

Concepts Statement No. 4 refers to the need for information about organization performance [¶47], resource flows related to operations [¶49], and service efforts and accomplishments [¶51–¶53]. This suggests that if the FASB had defined net income in a nonbusiness organization, the definition would correspond to its concept of net income in a business.

GASB Concept: Interperiod Equity

The GASB calls its corresponding concept "measurement of interperiod equity," which it defines as follows:

> Financial reporting should provide information to determine whether current-year revenues were sufficient to pay for current-year services. This also implies that financial reporting should show whether current-year citizens received services but shifted part of the payment burden to future-year citizens; whether previously accumulated resources were used up in providing services to current-year citizens; or, conversely, whether current-year revenues were not only sufficient to pay for current-year services, but also increased accumulated resources [GASB Cod. Sec. 100.177(a)].

The term "pay for" in this paragraph implies cash-basis accounting, but elsewhere (especially, in its Exposure Draft of December 15, 1987, *Measurement Focus and Basis of Accounting*), the GASB makes clear that it actually means accrual accounting.

Moreover, the statement does not refer specifically to the situation in which an organization, in the current period, uses capital that has been accumulated from surpluses in prior periods. It seems to me that the general thrust of the GASB position is that such an organization has not broken even in the current period. It breaks even only if its revenues are sufficient to restore the accumulated surplus to its former amount. Operating at a deficit may be good management, especially if it represents the use of a surplus for the "rainy day" contingency for which it presumably was accumulated. Nevertheless, the operating statement should not conceal the fact that there *was* a net loss in that year.

The concept of interperiod equity is entirely consistent with the business concept of net income described here. The organization breaks even if revenues just equal expenses. Capital contributions, such as capital assets contributed by another organization, are not revenues because they are not available to pay for the expenses of the current period.[22]

Significance of Net Income

Although the *measurement* of net income is the same, there is a difference in the *significance* of net income in business and nonbusiness organizations. Both businesses and nonbusinesses must be "financially viable," to use the term in FASB Concepts Statement No. 4 [¶14]. In order to be financially viable, a business must earn enough net income to satisfy its equity investors. A nonbusiness organization does not have equity investors and therefore is financially viable if its net income is somewhat greater than zero. (It needs some cushion to provide for possible "rainy days" and to provide equity funds for working capital purposes.)[23] Moreover, as a general rule, the larger the net income of a business the better its performance, whereas a large net income for a nonbusiness organization indicates that it did not provide as much service as it could have with available resources. In both business and nonbusiness organizations, a succession of net losses leads to bankruptcy. As the FASB states:

> A nonbusiness organization cannot, in the
> long run, continue to achieve its operating objec-

tives unless the resources made available to it at least equal the resources needed to provide services at levels satisfactory to resource providers and other constituents. [Information about this objective is] based at least partly on evaluations of past performance [CON 4 ¶39].

SPECIFIC ISSUES

In its meeting of March 17, 1986, the FASB discussed five "pervasive standards questions" relating to nonprofit organizations. Three are relevant to income measurement: depreciation, income from investments, and contributions. These and other items are discussed in the following paragraphs. In each case, I maintain that the proper treatment of these items is based on generally accepted principles of accrual accounting that should govern transactions in all organizations, business and nonbusiness.

Depreciation

By far the most controversial topic in the measurement of net income in nonbusiness organizations is depreciation. Indeed, the accounting concepts in the Governmental Accounting Standards Board Exposure Draft on *Measurement Focus and Basis of Accounting* differ from business accounting principles primarily with respect to this one item. Depreciation accounting is defined as:

> a system of accounting which aims to distribute the cost or other basic value of tangible capital assets, less salvage (if any), over the estimated useful life of the unit (which may be a group of assets) in a systematic and rational manner. It is a process of allocation, not of valuation [ARB 43, Ch. 9(C) ¶5].

Depreciation, as so defined, is a necessary element in the measurement of the maintenance of financial capital. If, over the life of an asset, revenues are not sufficient to recover all expenses, including the cost of the asset, the organization has not maintained its financial capital.

The sum of the annual depreciation charges, plus or minus the loss or gain on the disposition of the asset, does equal the asset's cost.

Exhibit 1 demonstrates the relevance of depreciation in measuring the maintenance of financial capital. The assumed situation is as follows: a nonbusiness organization purchased an item of equipment in 1981 for $1 million; the asset has a useful life of 10 years with no salvage value; the $1 million was obtained by borrowing, and there is $50,000 of annual interest cost. Prior to this purchase, the organization maintained its financial capital; that is, its net income was zero. It is able to increase its revenues by $150,000 a year, which recovers the cost of the asset plus interest over the 10 years. Thus, it continues to maintain its financial capital.

The asset can be accounted for in one of three ways: (1) depreciate the asset in accordance with the above definition; (2) capitalize the asset but do not depreciate it; or (3) write off the cost of the asset in the year of purchase.

Part A of Exhibit 1 demonstrates that depreciation is the best alternative. Net income remains at zero in each of the 10 years. At the end of the tenth year, the balance sheet returns to its previous state: the debt has been repaid, and the equipment has a book value of zero.[24]

Part B shows what would happen if the asset were capitalized but not depreciated. Reported net income would increase by one-tenth of the asset's cost each year; this report would say that the organization more than maintained its financial capital, which is incorrect. At the end of the tenth year, the balance sheet would show $1 million of equipment and an increase of $1 million in equity; both are incorrect. (If the asset were disposed of at the end of the tenth year and its costs were written off, this error would not occur.)

Part C shows what would happen if the asset were written off in the year of purchase. Reported net income would decrease by $1 million in that year, which is incorrect because the asset was not an expense of that year; the equipment provides service over 10 future years, and the cost is applicable to those years. The organization's equity would decrease by $1 million in the year of pur-

EXHIBIT 1 *ACCOUNTING FOR DEPRECIABLE ASSETS*

(000 omitted)

A. CORRECT REPORTING, AS IN BUSINESS GAAP

Balance Sheet	1/1/81	12/31/81	12/31/91
Cash	$ 800	$ 800	$ 800
Equipment	0	1,000	0
Other assets	5,200	5,200	5,200
Total assets	6,000	7,000	6,000
Debt	$ 0	$1,000	$ 0
Other liabilities	5,500	5,500	5,500
Equity	500	500	500
Total liabilities & equity	6,000	7,000	6,000

Operating Statement	1981	1982–91 (Each year)
Revenues	$2,000	$2,150
Expenses	2,000	2,150
Net Income	0	0

B. INCORRECT REPORTING, NO DEPRECIATION

Balance Sheet	1/1/81	12/31/81	12/31/91
Cash	$ 800	$ 800	$ 800
Equipment	0	1,000	1,000!
Other assets	5,200	5,200	5,200
Total assets	6,000	7,000	7,000
Debt	$ 0	$1,000	$ 0
Other liabilities	5,500	5,500	5,500
Equity	500	500	1,500!
Total liabilities & equity	6,000	7,000	7,000

Operating Statement	1981	1982–91 (Each year)
Revenues	$2,000	$2,150
Expenses	2,000	2,050
Net income	0	100!

C. INCORRECT REPORTING, IMMEDIATE WRITE-OFF

Balance Sheet	1/1/81	12/31/81	12/31/91
Cash	$ 800	$ 800	$ 800
Equipment	0	0	0
Other Assets	5,200	5,200	5,200
Total assets	6,000	6,000	6,000
Debt	$ 0	$1,000	$ 0
Other liabilities	5,500	5,500	5,500
Equity	500	(500)!	500
Total liabilities & equity	6,000	6,000	6,000

Operating Statement	1981	1982–91 (Each year)
Revenues	$ 2,000	$2,150
Expenses	3,000!	2,050!
Net Income	(1,000)!	100!

chase, which is incorrect because in fact the organization had a new asset exactly offset by an increase in a liability, so there was no effect on equity. Reported net income would increase by $100,000 in each of the next 10 years. This is incorrect because there is no recognition that the asset provided a service which increased the cost in each of these years.

In summary, depreciation on fixed assets acquired with operating resources is necessary to report whether financial capital has been maintained. If the fixed asset acquisition was financed with accumulated surpluses from prior years, depreciation shows, over the life of the asset, whether revenues are adequate to restore this surplus to its former position. If the acquisition was financed with debt, depreciation shows whether revenues were adequate to pay off the principal of the debt.

Other Reasons for Depreciation. Other arguments have been made for depreciating fixed assets acquired with operating resources. *They are not discussed here because the need to record depreciation in order to measure net income properly is a sufficient reason.* Statement No. 93 requires that assets be depreciated, and this requirement is sound with respect to operating assets, even though most of the rationale is irrelevant with respect to these assets. The arguments made in Statement No. 93 will be discussed in Part 3 on contributed capital. As I will show, depreciation on contributed capital assets is not relevant in measuring financial capital maintenance, and the justification for recording such depreciation must be on other grounds.

Alternatives to Depreciation. Rather than depreciate fixed assets acquired with operating resources, some nonbusiness organizations use the following alternatives: (1) they write off some fixed assets as an expenditure in the year of purchase, and/or (2) they record debt service principal payments as an expenditure for assets acquired with long-term debt.

If the amount of capital expenditures financed with currently available operating resources is approximately equal each year, then charging these expenditures to the current period will give approximately the same result as charging depreciation.[25] If the debt service principal payment is approximately equal to the depreciation amount, then using debt service principal as a surrogate for depreciation would also be satisfactory.[26] Therefore, both these alternatives should be permitted because they are in accordance with the materiality concept: an accounting method that approximates the conceptually correct method is acceptable.

However, these alternatives should be permitted only when they do approximate depreciation. Debt service schedules can easily be structured to shift the burden to future years. For example, repayment of principal may not start until several years after the asset was purchased, or there may be a large balloon payment in the final year of the debt. Such schedules result in an incorrect measure of the maintenance of financial capital. Organizations have been known to use them, however, as devices for hiding the real impact of fixed asset acquisitions on income in the early years (with the expectation that current management will not be around in the later years when the heavier burden is reported). Depreciation accounting will lessen management's ability to do this.

Note that the justification for these methods is that they approximate depreciation, not that they are inherently sound.

Investment Earnings

Many nonprofit organizations have endowments. Traditionally, the interest, dividend, and other income earned on these endowments were reported as revenues, and realized gains were added to endowment principal. In recent years, many organizations have adopted what is known as the "total-return/spending-rate" concept.

This concept is based on two ideas: (1) the total return on an equity investment typically is larger than the dividends received from such an investment; the total return includes the appreciation in the market value of the stock; but (2) only a portion of the total return should be considered as revenue of the current period, and the remainder should be added to the endowment principal to maintain its purchasing power. The amount booked as revenue is determined by applying a spending rate, approximately 5 percent, to the average market value of the endowment principal. This average is computed over a period of two or more prior years. Most states now permit the use of the total-return/spending-rate approach.

The total-return/spending-rate approach is similar to the approach in FASB Statement No. 87, *Employers' Accounting for Pensions,* even though the problem in pension accounting is to estimate the current *expense,* whereas the problem for endowments is to estimate the current *revenue.* In both cases, there is a focus on total return, a provision for using averages to reduce the impact of drastic changes in market value, and an estimate of the probable future rate of inflation.

The FASB approach to investment earnings, as implied in Concepts Statement No. 6, is inconsistent with this approach, however. As explained earlier, Statement No. 6 focuses on changes in net assets. Such a focus leads to a standard that records investment gains as increases in the current period (and, correspondingly, losses as decreases). The result would be wide fluctuations in the reported increase in net assets in years of large cyclical fluctuations in the stock market, even though these fluctuations are unrelated to management performance.[27]

The total-return/spending-rate approach is much sounder than the traditional approach or that implied in Concepts Statement No. 6. However, because many organizations continue to believe in the traditional approach, the standard at this time should probably permit either approach.

Contributions

Transactions involving contributions received from, or pledged by, outside parties are of course rare in businesses. Nevertheless, the general principles of income measurement suggest the solution of most such problems. By contrast, the concepts given in FASB Concepts Statement No. 6 lead to incorrect reporting of such transactions. This section discusses (1) pledges, (2) advance payments, and (3) contributions of personal services.

Pledges. At its meeting of June 22, 1988, the FASB decided that all unconditional pledges should be recognized in the period in which they are received. For the case of pledges of contributions for operating activities, this treatment is consistent with the matching concept because such pledges are usually made in response to an annual fund drive, and they are intended as revenues for the current period. The corresponding debit is to Pledges Receivable. Almost all will be paid during the period or shortly thereafter. Pledges judged to be uncollectible should be written off.

Pledges that are applicable to operations of a future period probably should not be entered in the accounts, for the same reason that sales orders for delivery in a future period are not entered in the accounts. No accounting entry is needed when such a pledge is received in order to measure the income of the current period.

Pledges to a capital campaign are a much different matter. These pledges will never become revenues; they do not affect the measurement of income in any period. When paid, the amount will be added to contributed equity as explained in Part 3. The benefit of reporting them on the balance sheet is minimal, and the amount that would be reported is extremely "soft" because of the uncertainty associated with pledges that are usually not due until several years later. Of course, careful records of such pledges should be maintained, and a report of the total amount of such pledges probably should be included in the Notes to the financial statements. Knowledgeable people recognize the softness of a number for pledges to a capital campaign, and believe it may give a misleading impression if included in the financial statements. They therefore will oppose the proposed treatment. The FASB's prestige will suffer if it requires recognition of such pledges in the accounts when such recognition serves no useful purpose and may even provide misleading information.

Advance Payments. Many businesses receive advance payments for goods to be delivered or services to be performed in future periods. Prepayment of magazine subscriptions is the example usually cited in textbooks. Such a prepayment creates a liability when the cash is received. The liability is discharged and revenue is recognized when the goods are delivered or the services are performed. Nonbusiness organizations also receive advance payments; that is, they receive money from a contributor who states that the contribution is to be used for some future purpose. For example, a college may receive a contribution of $50,000 in 1988 to finance a conference that is to be held in 1989.

In a business, such an advance payment would be recorded as a liability in 1988, and the liability would be discharged by a credit to revenue in 1989. By contrast, the FASB has stated that these payments, which it calls "temporarily restricted contributions," should be reported as an increase in net assets in the year of receipt, rather than in the year the services are performed [CON 6 ¶98 and ¶99].

This leads to an absurd operating statement. Using the same base situation as in Exhibit 1 (i.e., an organization that just maintains its financial capital with revenues of $2 million and expenses of $2 million), and assuming that the conference was held in 1989 at a cost of $50,000, the 1988 and 1989 operating statements under the FASB approach would be as follows:

(000 omitted)	1988	1989
Revenues	$2,050	$2,000
Expenses	2,000	2,050
Income	$ 50	$ (50)

The organization would report income of $50,000 in 1988, even though it had done nothing to earn the income and even though it had an obligation to hold the conference. It would report a loss of $50,000 in 1989, even though the cost of holding the conference was entirely offset by the contribution. It would report volative income when in fact the income was the same in both years.

During the years when the FASB devoted few resources to developing standards for nonbusiness organizations, the staff's attention was focused primarily on contributions. The nonbusiness task force tried to show the absurdity of the above presentation, without success.

Initially, the staff argued: the $50,000 isn't a liability in 1988 because if the conference isn't held, the organization might not be required to refund the money. This seemed to me to indicate a low opinion of the ethical standards of nonprofit managers.

In the final version of Concepts Statement No. 6, the rationale was: the advance payments are not available for payments to creditors, as long as the restriction remains [CON 6 ¶98]. This statement is clearly incorrect. Advance payments add to cash, and the pool of cash can be used to pay any bills. The FASB failed to distinguish between "restrictions on resources," the cash, and "restrictions on the use of resources," the obligation to hold the conference. As I will show in Part 3, capital contributions restrict both the actual resources and the use that can be made of these resources.

This distinction between business and nonbusiness accounting is unwarranted. Nonbusiness organizations should treat advance payments the same way businesses do—as liabilities until the period in which the obligation is discharged. The amount of the liability is useful information to creditors. Strangely, the Financial Accounting Foundation—the nonprofit parent of the Financial Accounting Standards Board—does treat advance payments for its publications as liabilities in its published financial statements, Concepts Statement No. 6 notwithstanding. Evidently, the parent is not impressed by the reasoning of its child.

Contributions of Personal Services. Under no circumstances do contributions of personal services affect the measurement of income. If they are recognized as revenues, the same amounts are simultaneously recognized as expenses, with no effect whatsoever on the bottom line. Recognition affects only the amount of expenses reported for individual programs or functions. Some years ago, hospitals and educational organizations received nursing, faculty, and other services from members of religious orders; they reported the value of these donated services on their operating statement. Currently, however, most religious orders bill the recipients for these services, so they are no longer contributions. It would be possible to calculate the value of the services rendered by trustees and other volunteers, but the benefits of doing so seem to be minimal, and the recordkeeping costs would be substantial. The sensible solution is to recognize the contributions of personal services only if they at least meet the stringent criteria spelled out in Statement of Position 78-10.[28]

Expenditure versus Expense

Some nonbusiness organizations report expenditures rather than expenses. Expenditures are decreases in assets or increases in liabilities that result from the *acquisition* of goods or services in a given period. Expenses are decreases in equity resulting from *consumption* during the period, that is, the using up of goods and services. Expenditures can result in either expired costs or unexpired costs. If the cost associated with an expenditure has expired during the period (as is usually the case for expenditures for labor and other services), the expenditure is also an expense. If the cost associated with an expenditure is unexpired during the period, it is an asset as of the end of the period. Such assets usually will become expenses in future periods.

In business accounting, expenses, rather than expenditures, enter into the measurement of net income. If nonbusiness organizations also reported expenses, their financial statements would be consistent with those of business and hence more understandable. However, the difference in treatment affects relatively few items.

For all personal service costs in nonmanufacturing organizations (salary, pension and other fringe benefits, payroll taxes, and contractual services), the services are consumed in the period in which they are acquired, so expenditures are the same as expenses. (In manufacturing companies, some of these costs are held in inventory until the product is sold.)

For inventories of consumable items, an expenditure is made when an item is added to inventory, whereas an expense is incurred in the period in which the item is consumed, which may be a later period. If inventory remains at approximately the same level from one period to the next, expenditures are approximately the same as expenses. The same reasoning applies to prepayments, such as prepaid insurance and prepaid rent. Also, the "initial outfit" principle permits initial acquisitions such as kitchen and dining room equipment, books in a library, or certain tools and dies to be capitalized, with replacements charged as expenses. Many businesses write off minor items when the expenditure is made, even though this is not strictly in accordance with the accrual concept; they reason that the extra work of tracing the item through to its consumption is not worthwhile. If, but only if, the difference is immaterial, these practices should not be criticized.

Other Differences in Income Measurement

I have described differences in the measurement of net income for business and nonbusiness organizations.[29] Major differences are (1) businesses use depreciation accounting, but many nonbusiness organizations do not, and (2) businesses use the expense basis, but many nonbusiness organizations use the expenditure basis. There are various minor differences. For example, the Governmental Accounting Standards Board has indicated that it may differ with the Financial Accounting Standards Board on certain aspects of pension accounting, although the pension expense of a government employee is no different from that of a business employee. Such differences reflect differences in personal judgment. A majority of the FASB voted one way, but a majority of the GASB may vote another way. The existence of such differences is unfortunate, but they are inevitable when two groups of individuals wrestle with the best accounting treatment of the same type of transaction. The solution is a single standards-setting body for similar transactions.

Conclusion

The primary focus of accounting in both business and nonbusiness accounting is on the measurement of net income so as to report an organization's success in maintaining its financial capital during an accounting period. The GASB calls this "interperiod equity." The FASB emphasizes this focus for business accounting, but it has not specifically addressed the problem of income measurement for nonbusiness organizations. Instead, it focuses on a concept that it calls "changes in net assets." This is not a useful concept. It mixes together income, which arises from operating activities, and changes in contributed capital, which are not associated with an organization's performance during an accounting period.

Although significant differences in measurement standards now exist among nonbusiness organizations of various types and between business and nonbusiness organizations, none of these reflects inherent differences in the concept of income measurement. Rather, they are explained by tradition and by the judgments of individual members of standards-setting bodies. The GASB's present plans would make government accounting consistent with business accounting, except for the treatment of depreciation; the GASB's rationale for a special treatment of depreciation is weak. The FASB seems to have gone out of its way to state differences that do not in fact exist.

The principles for the measurement of net income should be the same in organizations of all types.

Depreciation expense on depreciable assets acquired with an organization's operating resources, including borrowings, should be reported. This is necessary to measure the maintenance of financial capital, which is a sufficient reason.

3

Contributed Capital

In my 1978 report to the FASB, I listed the problem of separating operating inflows from capital inflows as the first major issue to be addressed. I prefaced the discussion with the following quote from the 1938 book by Sanders, Hatfield, and Moore [Anthony 1978, p. 71]:

> The distinction between capital and income, which everyone recognizes and the economist attempts to state with refined accuracy, is fundamental in accounting. Making effective and effectively maintaining as near as may be the distinction between the capital and income of a particular enterprise are the ultimate objectives that determine the activities of accountants and the functions of accounting.[30]

There are three aspects to this distinction. The first is the distinction between expenditures that should be capitalized and those that should be expensed. The second is the distinction between items that should enter into the measurement of net income and items that should be charged or credited directly to equity. The third is the distinction between operating inflows and capital inflows. This Part is limited to the third distinction.

Although the FASB has admitted that this distinction

exists [CON 4 ¶49], its existence has had no influence whatsoever on the FASB's conclusions about concepts and standards for nonbusiness accounting. In my opinion, its failure to consider this distinction is the primary cause of its unsatisfactory treatment of nonbusiness accounting issues. If the FASB took account of the distinction between operating inflows and capital inflows, its concepts would be essentially the same as those that govern business accounting.

Sources of Equity Capital

Business enterprises obtain equity capital from two sources: (1) retained earnings, which is an internal source; and (2) equity investors, which is an external source. The amount obtained from equity investors is listed on the balance sheet as paid-in capital. Although there are differences of opinion as to exactly where the line between these sources should be drawn, the distinction is clear enough for the present purpose.[31]

Basically, retained earnings consist of the cumulative total of the enterprise's net income from its inception, less dividends. As demonstrated in Part 2, net income should be measured according to the same principles in both nonbusiness and business organizations. The only difference in retained earnings, therefore, is that a nonbusiness organization does not pay dividends. (I prefer "operating equity" because "retained earnings" is an inappropriate term for nonbusiness organizations; they do not generate earnings as such.)

Paid-in capital is supplied by equity investors. The amount supplied is reported in the equities section of the balance sheet. The receipt of additional funds from equity investors does not increase net income or retained earnings, nor does the return of paid-in capital to equity investors reduce net income or retained earnings. Dividends paid to equity investors do not affect the measurement of income. In short, none of these capital transactions affects the measurement of income.

Although nonbusiness organizations do not have equity investors, they do receive equity capital from an external source. I shall use "contributed capital" as the name for this source. I define it broadly to include bequests for capital purposes; resources received in a capital campaign; capital appropriations made by a state to municipalities, universities, and other organizations for nonoperating purposes; and grants and contracts that specify payment for the acquisition of fixed assets. A few business organizations also receive contributed capital, usually from a municipality as an inducement to locate a plant there. In the accounting literature, contributed capital is treated as distinct from paid-in capital and similar to capital contributions in nonbusiness organizations.

Distinction Between Operating and Capital Contributions

An accounting standard that draws the line between operating contributions and capital contributions is needed. Until such a standard is published, we must rely on practice because many practical situations arise in which such a line must be drawn. For example, a nonprofit organization may seek operating contributions continuously, but it may undertake a capital campaign only every five or ten years. It must have rules that classify contributions so that those who manage the capital campaign can receive proper credit. In general, these rules provide that contributions are presumed to be operating contributions unless there is good evidence to the contrary. If the donor specifically states that the contribution is for the capital campaign, this is, of course, sufficient evidence. In the absence of an explicit statement, a contribution that is so large that it obviously was not intended for operating purposes, or a contribution that does not provide funds to meet operating expenses (such as works of art that are to be added to a museum collection) is classified as a capital contribution. Even when there is no capital campaign, large bequests and contributions of plant are counted as capital contributions.

As is the case with all classification schemes, there are borderline situations, and these often must be referred to the trustees for resolution. (A contribution that is not specifically designated as endowment but that is classified by the trustees as endowment is called "quasi endowment." Quasi endowment is contributed capital.)

Similar problems arise in government organizations. In the case of capital appropriations to be financed from nonoperating sources, or grants for plant or equipment that a municipality receives from the state or federal government, the distinction is reasonably clear. If a grant or contract is primarily for operating purposes, but some part of it may be used to acquire equipment, the classification is debatable. The important point is that if an asset acquisition is written off as an expense of the period, it cannot also be capitalized and depreciated; this would be double counting. Conversely, if the asset is treated as contributed capital, the corresponding part of the grant cannot be reported as revenue of the period; this would overstate income. The accounting treatment of a fixed asset acquisition that is financed partly with operating resources and partly with a capital grant or contract is discussed in a later section.[32]

The problem of drawing a line between operating contributions and capital contributions resembles the problem of drawing a line between debt capital and equity capital in a business. The general idea is clear: debt capital is a liability; equity capital is not. The application of this general idea to the variety of financial instruments that have been developed in recent years is the subject of much discussion and controversy.

Similarity of Contributed Capital to Paid-in Capital

Does contributed capital resemble paid-in capital more closely than it resembles retained earnings? I think it does. If it does, then inflows of contributed capital should not affect the amount of income reported in the current, or any, accounting period, just as inflows of paid-in capital never affect the measurement of income. The question is therefore central to the entire analysis.

Consider the resemblance between capital contributions in a nonbusiness organization and paid-in capital in a business. In both cases, the organization is better off by the amount of capital received. Unlike debt capital, additional equity capital does not involve a corresponding liability to repay. Although equity investors expect a return on their investment, the business does not promise them a return, nor is it obligated to provide one. Indeed, because the dividend yield in a typical company is much lower than the interest rate on that company's debt, it is clear that investors do not provide equity capital with the expectation of receiving more dividends than they could obtain from an investment in less risky bonds. They invest in equity primarily with the expectation that they can eventually sell the stock at a higher price than they paid for it. The gain from this sale comes from other investors who buy the stock, not from the business. The sales transaction has no effect on the accounts of the business.

The capital obtained from operating activities is obtained at a cost, as measured by operating expenses. Capital obtained from equity investors and capital obtained from contributors are also obtained at a cost. For equity capital, it is the cost associated with issuing capital stock. For contributed capital, it is fund-raising cost, the cost of preparing and selling contract proposals or capital budget requests, and similar marketing efforts. In both cases, the cost per dollar of capital obtained is much less than the cost of obtaining a dollar of net income. (Costs incurred in a capital fund-raising campaign should be reported as decreases in contributed equity, just as issuance costs of stock are deducted from paid-in capital. The measurement of income is unaffected in either case.)

As the FASB points out [CON 6 ¶137], both contributions by owners and contributions by nonowners are "nonreciprocal transfers," that is, transactions in which the organization receives something valuable but does not supply an asset or incur a liability of equal amount in exchange.

A difference between the two sources of capital is that equity investors are owners, whereas capital contributors are not owners. This is the sole reason why the FASB classifies contributed capital as a form of income rather than something that is distinct from income. As owners, equity investors have a claim on the organization's assets in the event of liquidation, whereas capital contributors have no such claim. To me, this distinction seems less important than the similarities discussed in the preceding paragraphs. According to the going-concern concept, the financial statements are based on the assumption that the organization is not about to be liquidated. That being the case, the fact that the owners have a claim is irrelevant. Even if the organization were liquidated, the amount that shareholders would receive has no relationship to the amount reported as shareholders' equity, except by coincidence; the reported amount therefore does not measure the owners' claim. Paid-in capital reports what equity investors have paid in, just as contributed capital reports what contributors have paid in. The reported amount is not the amount of a claim in either case.

Some people assert that the organization has an "obligation" to its owners, but not to its contributors. This assertion is wrong on two counts. First, the organization has no legal obligation to its owners. In a going concern, it has no obligation at all. In the event of liquidation, the owners don't get anything until all claims have been satisfied. If there were a legal obligation, accounting would require that owners' equity, or some part of it, be classified as a liability, which obviously is not the case. Second, management has a moral obligation to look out for the best interest of the owners, and it also has a moral obligation to used contributed resources prudently.

Another difference is that contributed equipment, buildings, and other plant items have a limited life, whereas paid-in capital remains on the books indefinitely. This difference does exist, and it is taken into account in the analysis that follows. It is of trivial importance compared with the similarities.

Section 1.118-1 of the Internal Revenue Code states that contributions to the capital of a corporation are not income and that property acquired with cash contribution by a nonshareholder cannot be depreciated for tax purposes. This distinction is borne out in many court cases. Although financial accounting is not governed by income-tax regulations or court cases, the reasoning in these sources is persuasive.

Many people who are familiar with business accounting have difficulty accepting the conclusion that contributed capital is not income. Basically, they emphasize the fact that these contributions make the organization "better off," without recognizing that contributions from owners also make the organization better off.

GASB Position

The GASB agrees that a capital contribution is not income. Its Measurement Focus Exposure Draft [¶59] states: "If an organization receives a donation of a capital asset, a capital expenditure should be recognized equal to the donation revenue recognized." Presumably, this means that even if the asset is not purchased or built in the period in which the revenue is recognized, the offsetting expenditure amount is held in a separate fund. Alternatively, the revenue could be recognized only when the asset is acquired. In any event, the revenue amount in a period is always equal to the expenditure amount, so there is no net effect on income.

FASB Position

In Concepts Statement No. 4 [¶49], the FASB emphasized the importance of the distinction between operating transactions and capital transactions:

> Financial reporting should provide information about the relation between inflows and outflows of resources during a period. Those who provide resources to a nonbusiness organization and others want to know how and why net resources changed during a period. To meet that need, *financial reporting must distinguish between resource flows that are related to operations and those that are not.* In this way, financial reporting may provide information that is useful in assessing whether the activities of a nonbusiness organization during a period have drawn upon, or contributed to past or future periods. Thus, it should show the relation of resources used in operations of a period to resource inflows available to finance those operations. Similarly, it should provide information

53

about changes in resources that are not related
to operations. For example, resource providers
to colleges or universities need information
about changes in an organization's endowment
and plant to understand more fully the changes
in its net resources during a period. [Emphasis
added; footnotes omitted.]

This is substantially the same as the interperiod equity concept that the GASB accepts as governing the
measurement of income. Note that in the above statement, endowment and plant, which are two principal
types of contributed capital, are specifically distinguished from resources related to operations.

Notwithstanding this paragraph in Concepts Statement No. 4, Concepts Statement No. 6 is silent about the
distinction between resource flows that are related to
operations and those that are not. Instead, Concepts
Statement No. 6 says that contributions of all types
should be recorded as revenues (or gains) in the period
in which they are received [CON 6 ¶103–¶107, ¶113, and
accompanying diagram]. To the FASB, inflows of contributed capital are not capital. They have the same effect on "changes in net assets" as revenues from tuition,
patients, clients, or other sources. (Remember that the
FASB never uses the term "income" for nonbusiness organizations; its closest term is "changes in net assets.")

Three Classes of Inflows. Rather than drawing a line
between operating flows and capital flows, the FASB
divided resource inflows into three "classes": unrestricted, temporarily restricted, and permanently
restricted [CON 6 ¶90–¶96]. The history of this classification is illuminating. In the July 1983 Exposure Draft of
what became Concepts Statement No. 6, the FASB
proposed a new financial statement element, "contributions." This element lumped together contributions of all
types, from annual dues to endowments, and as a result
there was strong opposition to it. In September 1985,
two years later, the FASB issued a revised Exposure Draft
in which it did away with the separate element and instead proposed three "classes" of contributions as sub-
divisions of equity (which it called "net assets"). The idea

of a "class" that was a subcategory of an element was new, and the nature of "classes" in a structure that was supposed to define "elements" remained murky. As is often the case with compromises, this one satisfied practically no one. Nevertheless, the revised Exposure Draft was adopted in December 1985 (one month after the deadline for comments) with only minor changes.

The FASB classification does not correspond to the conventional classification of operating inflows and capital inflows, and it cannot be made to fit this classification. This is indicated by the following diagram:[33]

Classification of Resource Inflows	
FASB	**CONVENTIONAL**
Unrestricted	Operating (Revenues) (Excludes plant)
Temporarily restricted*	Capital (Including plant)
Permanently restricted	
*Conventional treats this as a liability	

Most unrestricted resource inflows are operating revenues, but the FASB also includes contributed plant, which is a capital contribution, in this category, presumably because the donor placed no restrictions on the use that could be made of the plant. The FASB includes advance payments that will finance future operating activities in the temporarily restricted category, whereas conventional accounting treats these payments initially as a liability. They become revenue when expenses are incurred for the specified purpose. The FASB also classifies funds contributed for the purpose of acquiring plant as temporarily restricted until the plant has been acquired, when they become unrestricted; they are clearly capital contributions. The temporarily restricted class, therefore, contains a mixture of both operating and capital items. Permanently restricted contributions are capital contributions, but contributed plant is also a capital contribution.

Concepts Statement No. 6 does say [¶106] that "whether it [a nonprofit organization] has maintained certain classes of net assets may be more significant than whether it has maintained net assets in the aggregate." Separate reports would indeed be useful if there were a one-to-one correspondence between an FASB "class" and the conventional "operating" and "capital" categories. As I have indicated, there is no such correspondence. Such a classification scheme has never appeared previously in accounting, and I doubt that it ever will appear. It serves no useful purpose. It draws attention away from the fundamental task of accounting, which is to separate operating inflows from capital inflows so as to arrive at a correct measurement of net income.

Probably because of this mixed-up approach, the FASB did not specifically address the fundamental issue. The following syllogism gives its reasoning:

Major Premise: As stated in Concepts Statement No. 3, *Elements of Financial Statements of Business Enterprises,* the sources of equity capital are (1) retained earnings, and (2) contributions by owners.

Minor Premise: Contributed capital does not come from owners.

Conclusion: Therefore, it must affect retained earnings. Q.E.D.

The fallacy of this syllogism is that its major premise is incorrect. Although capital in business enterprises does come from either retained earnings or contributions from owners, capital in nonbusiness organizations comes from operating activities and capital contributions. A valid syllogism therefore is:

Major Premise: In a nonbusiness organization, the sources of equity capital are operating activities and capital contributions.

Minor Premise: Contributions of endowment and plant are capital contributions.

Conclusion: Therefore, these contributions should not be included as operating activities.

As pointed out earlier, the FASB states that capital contributions by both owners and nonowners are "nonreciprocal transfers." Accounting Principles Board Opinion No. 29 makes the same statement. Nothing in that opinion suggests that nonreciprocal transfers from nonowners should be treated as revenue. All the oft-cited ¶16 says is that contributed assets should be valued at their fair market value when they are initially booked. It says nothing whatsoever about treating these contributions as revenues. Nevertheless, the FASB classified capital contributions as revenues or gains [CON 6 ¶151], but it classified owners' contributions as something unrelated to revenues or gains. This is illogical.

Because the FASB's classification does not separate operating transactions from capital transactions, the FASB does not deal with operating transactions as a topic, and it does not discuss the measurement of income, since income is related solely to operating activities. Thus, the FASB is silent about the measurement of income in nonbusiness organizations, even though it states that the amount of income is an important indication of an organization's performance. As I pointed out in Part 2, most authorities regard income measurement as the most important objective of financial accounting, and most users of financial statements pay more attention to the income statement than to the balance sheet. The FASB never uses the word "income" in its discussion of nonbusiness organizations; the word does not fit its classification scheme. Instead it uses the vague "changes in net assets." Nor can the FASB admit that income is the "primary focus" of accounting in nonbusiness organizations as is the case in businesses; with its classification structure, income is not a focus at all.

The FASB staff has developed a complicated set of journal entries that transfer items back and forth between its three classes. These have not been made public. Journal entries that would ultimately produce the equivalent of a net-income amount conceivably could be constructed. Since the three classes are not useful, it would be much better to make the entries to either operating or capital accounts as the transactions occur.

Practical Consequences

So far, my discussion has been primarily conceptual. Conceptual nuances are, of course, less important than their practical consequences. Does the FASB approach result in meaningful financial statements? I don't believe that it does. In the following paragraphs, I shall discuss the two main types of contributed capital—endowment and plant—and contrast the correct approach with the approach that follows from Concepts Statement No. 6.

Endowment. Consider a contribution in the form of an ordinary endowment. The organization cannot legally use the principal of such a contribution to finance its operating activities, but it benefits from the earnings on that principal. Endowment principal is therefore not an item of revenue in the year in which it is received, or indeed in any year. Moreover, the assets in which the endowment is invested must be segregated from operating assets. They are not legally available to pay operating bills. An operating statement that included endowment principal as revenue would be grossly misleading: the amount could mask an operating deficit. A balance sheet that mingled endowment assets with operating assets would be equally misleading.

Exhibit 2 illustrates this point. The beginning data and assumptions are the same as those in Exhibit 1. In the base case, the organization just breaks even; that is, its revenues equal its expenses, and it maintains its financial capital. Assume that in 1981 the organization received a contribution of $1 million as an endowment. It can use the earnings on the $1 million for operating purposes, but it never can use the principal. Further, assume that earnings on this endowment are $100,000 a year and that the organization accordingly increases its services by spending $100,000 more a year. (Donors who contribute endowment expect that the organization will make good use of the earnings; therefore they expect services to be increased.)

The correct reporting is in Part A of Exhibit 2. Income continues on a break-even basis each year. A balance sheet item, contributed equity, increased by $1 million in the year of receipt.

Part B shows how the transactions would be reported under the FASB approach. Income increased by $1 million in 1981, suggesting that the organization had operated so as to produce that amount of additional income and that this amount was available to finance

```
┌─────────────────────────────────────────────────────────────────────┐
```

EXHIBIT 2 ACCOUNTING FOR ENDOWMENT
(000 omitted)

A. CORRECT REPORTING

Operating Balance Sheet and Operating Statement
These statements are unaffected by contributed plant transactions.

Contributed Capital Balance Sheet

	1/1/81	12/31/81	12/31/91
Cash and securities	$0	$1,000	$1,000
Total assets	0	1,000	1,000
Contributed equity	0	1,000	1,000

Contributed Flow Statement

	1981	1982
Increases	$1,000	$100
Decreases	0	$100
Net Change	1,000	0

B. FASB METHOD

Balance Sheet

	1/1/81	12/31/81	12/31/91
Cash	$ 800	$1,800!	$1,800
Other assets	5,200	5,200	5,200
Total assets	6,000	7,000	7,000
Liabilities	5,500	5,500	5,500
Equity	500	1,500	1,500
Total liabilities & equity	6,000	7,000	7,000

Operating Statement

	1981	1982–90 (Each year)
Revenues	$3,000	$2,100
Expenses	2,000	2,100
Net Income	1,000!	0

```
└─────────────────────────────────────────────────────────────────────┘
```

operating activities. Actually, it cannot use the $1 million for operating purposes, and the organization would be foolish to increase its spending in 1981 by $1 million. The implication that management turned in an extraordinarily good performance in 1981 is misleading. The organization did receive additional resources in that year, but this receipt was in no way associated with the operations of 1981. The more realistic alternative is to report that the organization broke even each year. This can be accomplished by reporting the receipt of the endowment as contributed capital rather than as revenue. The implication that the organization's bill-paying ability increased by $1 million is also misleading. Using endow-

EXHIBIT 3 ACCOUNTING FOR CONTRIBUTED PLANT
(000 omitted)

A. CORRECT REPORTING

Operating Balance Sheet and Operating Statement
These statements are unaffected by contributed plant transactions.

Contributed Capital Balance Sheet

	1/1/81	12/31/81	12/31/91
Equipment	$0	$1,000	$0
Total assets	0	1,000	0
Contributed equity	$0	$1,000	$0

Contributed Flow Statement (Option 1)

	1981	1991
Increases	$1,000	$0
Decreases	0	1,000
Net change	1,000	(1,000)

Contributed Flow Statement (Option 2)

	1981	1982–91 (Each year)
Increases	$1,000	$0
Decreases	0	100
Net change	1,000	(100)

B. INCORRECT REPORTING

Balance Sheet

	1/1/81	12/31/81	12/31/91
Cash	$800	$800	$800
Equipment	0	1,000	0
Other assets	5,200	5,200	5,200
Total assets	6,000	7,000	6,000
Liabilities	$5,500	5,500	$5,500
Contributed equity	0	1,000	0
Operating equity	500	500	500
Total liabilities & equity	6,000	7,000	6,000

Operating Statement

	1981	1982–91 (Each year)
Revenues	$2,000	$2,000
Expenses	2,000	2,100
Net Income	0	(100)!

ment assets to pay operating bills is not only unwise, it is illegal.

Contributed Plant. The illustration can be made to parallel the situation in Exhibit 1 more closely by assuming that the organization received a contribution of a depreciable asset worth $1 million (or $1 million cash with the stipulation that it acquire such an asset). Assume, further, that the asset has a service life of 10 years.

If, as I maintain, this contribution is treated as contributed capital, the financial statements would be as

EXHIBIT 3 ACCOUNTING FOR CONTRIBUTED PLANT cont'd
(000 omitted)

C. INCORRECT REPORTING, INCREASED REVENUE

Balance Sheet	1/1/81	12/31/81	12/31/91
Cash	$800	$800	$1,800!
Equipment	0	1,000	0
Other assets	5,200	5,200	5,200
Total assets	6,000	7,000	7,000
Liabilities	$5,500	$5,500	$5,500
Contributed equity	0	1,000	0
Operating equity	500	500	1,500
Total liabilities & equity	6,000	7,000	7,000

Operating Statement	1981	1982–91 (Each year)
Revenues	$2,000	$2,100!
Expenses	2,000	2,100
Net income	0	0

D. ALTERNATIVE REPORTING (IASC 20)

Balance Sheet	1/1/81	12/31/81	12/31/91
Cash	$800	$800	$800
Equipment	0	1,000	0
Other assets	5,200	5,200	5,200
Total assets	6,000	7,000	6,000
Liabilities	$5,500	$5,500	$5,500
Contributed equity	0	1,000	0
Operating equity	500	500	500
Total liabilities & equity	6,000	7,000	6,000

Operating Statement	1981	1982–91 (Each year)
Revenues	$2,000	$2,100
Expenses	2,000	2,100
Net income	0	0

shown in Part A of Exhibit 3. The operating balance sheet and operating statement would not be affected. A separate set of financial statements would be prepared for the contributed plant. Its balance sheet would show the plant (equipment) asset at its cost of $1 million in 1981, with an offsetting amount for contributed equity. (As an alternative, the balance sheet could be a separate section of a combined balance sheet, but this is an unimportant variation in format.)

A flow statement would report the changes in contributed equity. (This statement should not be called an income statement or operating statement because it does not report revenues and expenses.) The flow statement report could be prepared in either of two ways. Option 1 assumes that reporting depreciation expense on this asset is not worthwhile. With this option, a flow statement in 1981 explains the increase in contributed capital, and another in 1991 explains the decrease in the amount of contributed capital when the asset is retired, but there are no capital flows in the intervening years.

Option 2 assumes that for some reason a report of the annual depreciation on this asset is worthwhile. For each year, 1982 through 1991, $100,000 of the asset cost would be written off and so reported on the contributed flow statement. The asset amount and the contributed equity account would be reduced accordingly.

Incorrect Reporting. If the capital aspects of these transactions were reported on the operating balance sheet and operating statement, the statements would be misleading.

One scenario is shown in Part B of Exhibit 3. This complies with the requirement of FASB Statement No. 93 that all assets should be depreciated. The 12/31/81 balance sheet would presumably show contributed equity separately from operating equity (i.e., the equity obtained by operating at a surplus in previous years); it would not be misleading. The addition of the $100,000 annual depreciation would result in $2,100,000 in annual expenses and a reported annual loss of $100,000 if there were no increase in revenue. In fact, there would be no loss; the $1 million asset did not cost the organization anything; there is no cost to recover. The organization has maintained its operating capital just as it did before the capital contribution.

If, in order to avoid a reported loss, the organization increased its prices by $100,000 a year, a peculiar thing would happen, as shown in Part C. The additional revenue would generate $100,000 additional cash annually, so that at the end of 10 years, the cash balance would grow by $1 million. Thus, the operating statement would say that the organization has only broken even, but the cash account would say, correctly, that the organization has more resources.

FASB Staff Reaction. When presented with the absurd reports illustrated in Parts B and C, the FASB staff may say, "We really didn't mean that depreciation expense on contributed plant should be subtracted from revenue." There are three things wrong with this way out. First, Statement No. 93 explicitly refers to depreciation *expense,* and expenses are subtracted from revenues by definition. Second, if depreciation is not reported on an operating statement, it cannot enter into the measurement of the cost of services, service effort, or stewardship, which are reasons given by the FASB for reporting depreciation. (Or, it can be incorporated only by a special study rather than by information drawn directly from the accounts.) Third, if the intention was that depreciation *not* be subtracted from revenue, the FASB easily could have said so. This would have avoided (or at least lessened) the clamor that has arisen about Statement No. 93.

An even more ingenuous staff justification is, "Your exhibits are matters of display, and in Concepts Statement No. 6 we deliberately excluded such matters. We have asked the AICPA to make recommendations on display." This is a cop-out. The operating statements in Exhibit 3 are not mere matters of display. They illustrate fundamental concepts regarding the measurement of income, which is a basic objective of accounting.

In brief, the FASB position makes no sense.

An Alternative Solution. Part D of Exhibit 3 shows the results if, instead of raising prices, the organization reported $100,000 of additional revenue a year and decreased both the asset and the contributed equity by the same amount. This is the practice recommended by International Accounting Committee (IASC) Standard No. 20, *Accounting for Government Grants and Disclosure of Government Assistance* [¶38]. The operating statement would then report that the organization broke even each year because the annual depreciation expense was financed by a past contribution, which is correct. The treatment in Part C implies that additional revenues are required in order to break even, which is incorrect. The

63

disadvantage of the IASC approach is that it requires additional recordkeeping, which is warranted only if the additional information is worthwhile. I will discuss this point next.

DEPRECIATION ON CONTRIBUTED CAPITAL ASSETS

As I explained in Part 2, depreciation on assets that an organization acquires with its own resources (including borrowings) must be recorded as an expense in order to measure income properly. An organization breaks even only when its revenues equal all its costs, including the costs incurred to acquire fixed assets, and the annual charge to recover this past cost is depreciation. Because this is a sufficient reason for recording depreciation on these assets, no other possible benefits of recording depreciation were discussed in Part 2.

Depreciation on contributed capital assets should not affect income. These assets had zero cost to the organization. The organization breaks even—maintains its financial capital—if its revenues at least equal all the costs that were actually incurred. The misleading consequences of charging depreciation are illustrated in Parts B and C of Exhibit 3.

One way of recording depreciation without affecting income is to subtract depreciation from the cost of the asset in a plant fund or similar set of accounts that is separate from the operating accounts, as illustrated in Part A (Option 2) of Exhibit 3. Although some organizations use this practice, it doesn't accomplish anything worthwhile. If the amount is simply listed as a subtraction from a plant fund, it cannot be combined with other expenses to provide measurements of costs that some believe to be an important benefit of recording depreciation. The net book value of a plant fund does not convey information that is of much use to anyone.

There is only one possibly useful way of recognizing depreciation on contributed capital assets on the operating statement without affecting net income. This is to report on the operating statement an item of contributed revenue that is exactly equal to the amount of depreciation expense, as recommended by IASC Statement No. 20 and illustrated in Part D of Exhibit 3. The IASC method involves additional accounting costs, and they may be substantial.[34] The issue is whether, or under what circumstances, the benefits of recording depreciation exceed the costs of doing so. This issue is discussed in the following paragraphs.

Note the fundamental difference in the analysis of the two types of depreciation. Depreciable operating assets *must* be depreciated in order to measure net income correctly; the organization has not broken even unless its revenues are sufficient to recover all its costs, including the costs it incurred in acquiring fixed assets. However, there is no need to inquire whether depreciation of these assets serves any other useful purpose. Depreciation on contributed capital assets is not needed to measure whether the organization has broken even. The work of recording depreciation on these assets is worthwhile only if the benefits of doing so are believed to exceed the cost.[35]

Some accountants instinctively reject the existence of this difference. To them, assets are assets, and depreciation expense writes off the cost of any and all depreciable assets. In their view, the idea of bringing nonbusiness accounting close to business accounting is compromised if depreciation is treated differently in the two types of organizations. The analysis made here will not persuade them to change their opinion unless they are willing to suspend this instinctive belief.[36]

Possible Benefits of Depreciation

The FASB is one of the few standards-setting bodies that requires that depreciation on contributed fixed assets be treated as an expense, thus decreasing the amount of reported net income. As I have noted, International Accounting Standard No. 20 states that depreciation on contributed capital assets should be recorded, but the amount should be offset by an equal amount of contributed revenue.[37] In its Measurement Focus Exposure Draft, the Governmental Accounting Standards Board proposes that the amount of contributed fixed assets be reported as revenue at the top of the operating statement and that the same amount be subtracted as an expenditure at the bottom, with no net effect on income [GASB Measurement Focus, ¶59]. Accounting principles for the federal government encourage, but do not require, depreciation on contributed assets.[38] If nonprofit organizations report depreciation on contributed assets at all, most report it as a subtraction within a plant fund, not as a charge against operations.

Nevertheless, there are possible benefits, and these are discussed below.[39] Some of them are stated in the FASB's "Basis for Conclusions" in Statement No. 93, and the paragraph numbers in parentheses at the beginning of some of the following paragraphs are references to that document. The FASB's basic position is that depreciation on operating assets need not be distinguished from depreciation on contributed assets [¶26–¶28].

Information Provided. In judging whether asserted benefits are worthwhile, the nature of the information that would be reported needs to be kept in mind. Most important, a standard would apply to the primary financial statements: the balance sheet and operating statement. (If depreciation is reported only as a Note or as supplementary information, it cannot be a component of expense and therefore will not affect the measurement of income or the cost of services.) Exhibit 4 shows the additional information that typically would be disclosed in the general-purpose financial statements if depreciation on contributed capital assets were reported.

The operating statement would report an item for depreciation expense, offset by an equal amount of revenue. Conceivably, the depreciation expense would be one of the cost elements for the individual programs that use depreciable assets, in order to provide a better measure of the actual cost of these program, but Statement No. 93 has no such requirement; only the total amount of depreciation expense for the period is required to be reported [¶5].

On the balance sheet, there would be a report of accumulated depreciation and the resulting net book value of all assets. Although the costs of broad asset classes (land, land improvements, buildings, and equipment) are shown separately, Statement No. 93 does not require that

EXHIBIT 4 *INFORMATION PROVIDED BY DEPRECIATION OF CONTRIBUTED CAPITAL ASSETS*
(Additional Information Underlined)

OPERATING STATEMENT
For Year Ended June 30, 1988 (000 omitted)

Revenues

Other revenues	$20,000
Capital contributions recognized	1,800
Total revenues	21,800

Expenses

Other expenses	20,000
Depreciation expense	1,800
Total expenses	21,800
Net income	$0

CONTRIBUTED CAPITAL BALANCE SHEET
As of June 30 (000 omitted)

Assets	**1988**	**1987**
Property, plant equipment		
Land	$1,000	$1,000
Land improvements	2,000	2,000
Buildings	40,000	40,000
Equipment	10,000	10,000
Gross book value	53,000	53,000
Less accumulated depreciation	21,800	20,000
Net book value	31,200	33,000
Endowment portfolio	25,000	25,000
Total assets	$56,200	$58,000
Liabilities and Equity		
Contributed plant	$31,200	$33,000
Contributed endowment	25,000	25,000
Total liabilities & equity	$56,200	$58,000

Note 1: Summary of Significant Accounting Policies
Depreciation. Depreciable assets are stated at cost.
Depreciation is calculated on a straight-line basis over estimated
useful lives. The estimated useful lives are 25 to 50 years for
buildings and improvements and 3 to 10 years for equipment.

accumulated depreciation for each class be reported.
Even if accumulated depreciation were reported for each
asset class, this is quite different from reporting accumulated depreciation for individual assets within a class.
Thus, at most, the balance sheet would show the *average*
percentage of cost that has been depreciated, which is an

indication of the average age of the assets in the class. More likely, it would show only the average percentage for all assets combined. The cost reported would be the historical cost, not the replacement cost or current market value. (Records maintained for insurance purposes show estimates of the replacement cost of individual assets, but these records are entirely separate from the asset amounts that are governed by accounting standards.)

Cost Comparisons. The principal reason for recording depreciation is to facilitate cost comparisons among organizations or among programs within an organization. Depreciation expense may allow for differences between an organization that owns its assets and an organization that leases them, or for differences between a program that is capital intensive and a program that does not use a significant amount of fixed assets. (Statement No. 93 does not even mention these possible uses.) However, the validity of such comparisons is dubious because of differences in the price level that affect the cost of assets acquired at different times, in the method of depreciation, in the estimate of service life, and other factors. Variations in these factors mean that the depreciation expense of $1,000 for one asset may not bear any relationship to the depreciation expense of $1,000 for another asset. Moreover, unless a standard requires that depreciation expense be assigned to individual programs, which is unlikely, even these comparisons cannot be made from the information provided in the general-purpose financial statements.

Some industry associations that collect costs from their members and compute averages for comparison purposes omit depreciation entirely; others require members to calculate a number that is unrelated to accounting depreciation. The Appendix of this monograph describes some of these industry cost comparisons. Those who believe that depreciation is useful for cost comparisons should provide specific, real-world examples.

Measure of Service Efforts. [FASB 93 ¶22 and ¶26]. Recording depreciation to measure service efforts relates to the previous point, and as was the case there, the argument would be much stronger if concrete examples of such use could be provided. My skepticism is based on the inherent limitation of the depreciation number.

Basis for Cost Reimbursement. Recording depreciation on the operating statement is usually not necessary as a condition for obtaining reimbursement under cost-type contracts. These contracts state whatever basis of reimbursement the parties agree to. In some, the buyer agrees to pay the cost of asset acquisitions. In others, there is a capital allowance calculated as a percentage of some asset number; this has no relation to accounting depreciation. Some contracts do provide reimbursement for book depreciation; if so, depreciation should of course be recorded. However, such reimbursement is likely to understate the current cost of using or replacing assets. Buyers who reimburse for depreciation on the grounds that doing so compensates for actual usage costs usually don't understand that book depreciation bears little relationship to current usage costs.

Questions can be raised about the ethics of a management that argues that the organization is entitled to reimbursement for depreciation on contributed assets. If the organization incurred no cost for the asset, and if the use of the asset for a certain project does not interfere with its use for other purposes, why is the organization entitled to reimbursement? The question is acute if the customer paid for the asset in the first instance, as is the case with many federal government contracts.

Differences in Types of Assets

The possible benefits of depreciation vary considerably with assets of different types. I cannot conceive of a use that would be made of depreciation on a cathedral, church, or synagogue acquired with contributed capital. The academic plants of colleges and universities are usually acquired with contributed capital if they are private and with capital appropriations if they are public, but I do not know of an instance in which the depreciation number has been used for any purpose. I suppose that depreciation on a nonprofit museum, hospital, aquarium, concert hall, or art gallery built with contributed capital might be used in cost comparisons with their for-profit counterparts, although I know of no evidence of such use.

These differences suggest that, at most, depreciation on contributed fixed assets should be optional. If an organization decides that depreciation is worthwhile, it should be permitted to report depreciation expense, with an equal amount added to revenue. Ideally, the FASB should establish criteria that would help in such a decision, but a revision of Statement No. 93 should not be delayed in order to develop such criteria.

None of these limitations prevents an organization from recording depreciation for internal purposes if it wants to do so. Financial accounting standards relate only to financial statements prepared for external users.

Fallacious Arguments for Depreciation

The arguments that follow are not, in fact, benefits of recording depreciation on contributed fixed assets. Depreciation will not produce any of these benefits. Most of these arguments are made by people who think depreciation is something that it is not. Depreciation merely writes off the historical cost of an asset, a cost that in some cases was booked many years ago. It is not a measure of current sacrifice that is remotely comparable with, say, the cost of materials consumed, of purchased labor and other services, or of prepayments.

All Costs Should Be Accounted For [FASB 93 ¶20]. The idea that all costs should be accounted for is, by all odds, the principal reason why many accountants believe that depreciation on contributed assets should be recorded. It is the theme of the FASB's "Basis for Conclusions" in Statement No. 93. The deeply held belief arises because in most situations accountants do attempt to discover and book costs.

As I have shown earlier in this Part, however, there is a whole class of costs that accountants do not record at all, or costs that they record in a way that does not affect the measurement of income. These are the costs associated with capital transactions. In a business, the cost of using equity capital is not recorded, even though there surely is such a cost; equity investors do not furnish capital for nothing. Economists recognize the cost of using equity capital; accountants do not. Dividends are recorded; they are a part of the cost of using equity capital, but they are not recorded as a charge that affects income measurement. Return of paid-in capital to shareholders similarly is not recorded as a cost to the corporation, even though this reduces its net assets. (Repayment of debt does *not* reduce net assets.) The issuance costs associated with issuing equity securities are not recorded as an expense in the income statement.

No accounting concept or standard states that all costs should be recorded. On the contrary, Concepts Statement No. 2 [¶133–¶146] emphasizes the point that accounting should report information only if the benefits of doing so exceed the associated costs. Accounting does not record opportunity costs (i.e., the income foregone by using resources for a certain purpose rather than for some other purpose), or implicit costs (e.g., the value of the time that trustees devote to the activities of a non-profit organization), or the asset amounts for goodwill or trade names that were not purchased.

There are two types of costs: unexpired costs and expired costs. Unexpired costs are assets, and accounting should report the cost of contributed capital assets. Expired costs are expenses. As explained in this Part, the depreciation expense of contributed capital assets is irrelevant in measuring the maintenance of financial capital, and its usefulness for other purposes is doubtful, at best.

Some people point out that Accounting Principles Board Opinion No. 29 says that contributed assets are to be recorded at their fair value. However, Opinion No. 29 does *not* say that contributed assets should be depreciated. In fact, the only example it gave was contributed land, which is not depreciated [¶6].

Indication of Service Potential [FASB 93 ¶24]. Some people argue that net book value is an indication of service potential. An asset with zero or relatively low book value is thought to have little future use. There is little evidence that such an indication is valid. More than 100 colleges and universities have buildings that were built before the Civil War. If these buildings had been depreciated, their book values would have reached zero many years ago. Many of them are in excellent condition. By contrast, many low-income housing units built by municipalities in recent years were shoddily constructed and are near the end of their useful life, even though, if depreciated, their net book value would be substantial. Moreover, as shown in Exhibit 4, accounting does not report the net book value of individual assets.

In its Discussion Memorandum on Capital Assets, the GASB used a report from the City of Dayton, Ohio, as an example of useful information. The information was interesting, but none of it came from historical accounting records of depreciable assets. The information either was nonmonetary or was an estimate of replacement costs.[40]

Reporting on Accountability [FASB 93 ¶18]. Depreciation does not facilitate reporting on how well management carried out its obligation to ensure that assets are properly safeguarded. Accountability is accomplished by the system for controlling individual assets through the maintenance of adequate property records and audits of these records.

Reporting on Management Performance [FASB ¶22]. Depreciation is a fraction of the cost of assets acquired at some time in the past. It has nothing to do with how well the current management used those assets.

It is often argued that management is responsible for obtaining contributed assets and that its success in doing this should be reported on the financial statements. This is so, but depreciation is not relevant in such a report. The contributed capital obtained during the year should be reported on the flow statement showing changes in contributed equity. Similarly, it is said that the financial statements should report management's performance in managing its resources. Within the inherent limitations of financial reporting, this is so; however, depreciation does not provide relevant information for this purpose.

Reporting on Stewardship. Interpretations of the meaning of "stewardship" in accounting vary. To some, it means accountability; to others, it means performance. In either case, the point is covered in the two preceding paragraphs.

Budget Planning. Depreciation does not facilitate

budget planning. It represents costs incurred in prior periods, and decisions made in the budget period have little effect on, and are not affected by, the depreciation expense of that period.[41]

Indication of Deferred Maintenance. Depreciation does not indicate whether an asset has been properly maintained. Accounting reports the amount actually spent on maintenance, but this is unrelated to depreciation. Deferred maintenance is a matter of great concern in many organizations, but depreciation does not indicate the amount that should be spent to maintain assets, nor does the difference between depreciation expense and actual maintenance cost measure deferred maintenance. Deferred maintenance is measured by engineers, not accountants. Furthermore, as Exhibit 4 illustrates, the financial statements do not report information on individual assets. It is inconceivable that a standards-setting body would require that such information would be reported. At most, depreciation on broad asset categories would be required, and not even this detail is required in business financial statements. The best way of finding out the condition of the plant is to look at it.

Indication of Replacement Costs. The original cost of depreciable assets does not indicate their replacement cost. Depreciation does not provide a fund for replacement, nor does the annual depreciation charge enter into estimates of cash needs. Depreciation pertains solely to assets that have been acquired in the past. An organization has maintained its financial capital if it recovers the cost of assets acquired with operating resources during their useful life. Future asset acquisitions are ultimately financed by future revenues. The fact that resources have been adequate to replace assets in the past is no indication that they will be adequate in the future. This point is sharpened by considering an asset that was financed with long-term debt. The annual debt principal payment, which may be an acceptable surrogate for depreciation, discharges the debt for the asset acquired in the past. It does not provide a fund for future asset acquisitions. Indeed, it has nothing whatsoever to do with the acquisition of future assets.

Similar Transactions Should Be Reported Similarly. Presumably, the idea behind this platitude is that cost comparisons should be comparable, and this is so. However, comparability is not necessary if the depreciation expense is not useful. For reasons given earlier, depreciation expense is rarely useful in cost comparisons. Moreover, contributed fixed assets are *not* similar to fixed assets acquired with operating resources. The latter involved a cost to the organization; the former had zero cost.

Assets Should Be Reported. This is so, and contributed plant should be reported on the contributed capital balance sheet. However, the net book value of plant (i.e., the gross cost less depreciation) is not a useful number. Both Standard & Poor's and Moody's, the two leading bond rating agencies, have stated that non-reporting of depreciation on the balance sheet will not affect the credit rating of private colleges and universities.[42] If rating experts have questions about the condition of the plant, they look at the plant.

Overstatement of Asset Values. If depreciation were not recorded, contributed assets would be carried at their acquisition cost, and this could be an overstatement of their current value. For reasons given earlier, however, carrying them at some fraction of that cost does not provide useful information.

Treatment of Partly Contributed Assets Would Be Confusing. It is true that the approach suggested above would result in depreciation on assets purchased with an organization's own resources, but not on contributed capital assets. If an asset were financed from both sources, the amount of depreciation would be understated. However, there is probably no use for the full amount, for reasons given earlier. Again, recall Exhibit 4: the balance sheet does not report the book value of individual assets, and therefore it does not reveal whether an individual asset was financed by operating resources, contributions, or a combination of both.

Moreover, if the federal government finances 50 percent of the cost of building a municipal sewer plant, the taxpayers or users shouldn't be asked to pay for this 50 percent; the purpose of the subsidy is to reduce the cost to them. If 100 percent of the cost were included as an expense and the tax rate were set to cover all expenses, taxpayers would be paying both for the 50 percent that must be recouped from revenues and also for the subsidized 50 percent.

Donors Should Have Their Contributions Recognized. Donor contributions are, of course, recognized but in ways that do not affect the financial statements.

CONCLUSIONS

Contributed Capital

Transactions relating to contributed capital in a nonbusiness organization should be kept entirely separate from transactions relating to the measurement of income, just as transactions relating to paid-in capital are kept separate from operating transactions in business accounting. This requires a separate balance sheet (or a separate section of a single balance sheet) that reports the amount of contributed equity and the assets associated with this equity.

The FASB approach does not do this, and its approach therefore does not measure income. Although it states that the measurement of income should be the primary focus in business accounting, the FASB doesn't even suggest that the measurement of income is important in a nonbusiness organization. In fact, income measurement is important in both business and nonbusiness organizations, and the accounting principles are the same for both types.

The FASB should disregard the classification of nonbusiness resources into three classes as specified in its Concepts Statement No. 6. Instead, it should focus on the separation of transactions into two types: operations and contributed capital.

Depreciation

Depreciation on assets acquired with an organization's own resources is necessary to measure net income, which reports how well the organization has maintained its financial capital through its operating activities. Depreciation on contributed capital assets is not useful for this purpose and will produce misleading results if permitted to influence the measurement of net income.

Depreciation on contributed assets may be beneficial in making cost comparisons and in measuring service effort, but there is little evidence that such benefits are worth the associated costs. Depreciation may be recorded when cost-reimbursement contracts require that reimbursement be based on book depreciation, but this is not a reason why all organizations should record depreciation. Other reasons advanced for recording depreciation on these assets are invalid.

At most, recording depreciation on contributed assets should be optional, and when depreciation is reported, an equal amount of revenue should be reported in the same period.

4

Financial Statements

S tandards-setting bodies have given little attention to the format and content of the general-purpose financial statements of nonbusiness organizations. The FASB has done nothing. The GASB has eliminated the requirement for a separate fund for special assessments [GASB Statement No. 6], and its Exposure Draft on Measurement Focus implies, but does not explicitly deal with, further simplification. Statement users who are not thoroughly familiar with nonbusiness accounting find the separate columns and sections of the typical financial statement confusing. Much of the confusion stems from the traditional use of a variety of separate funds.

In this Part, I describe how general-purpose financial statements can be made more understandable by eliminating unnecessary information about funds.[43]

Fund Accounting

A fund is a self-balancing group of accounts. Each fund is considered to be a separate "accounting entity"; that is, its total assets always equal its total liabilities plus equity. Although most nonbusiness textbooks imply that fund accounting is used primarily in nonbusiness organizations, this is not so. Businesses have pension funds, fiduciary funds, escrow funds, agency funds, and other funds that are entities separate from the business's own accounts. Funds are used by both business and nonbusiness organizations to facilitate control or because they are legally required.

Fund Structure in Government Accounting. The fund structure currently used in government organizations reflects an attempt in the 1960s to shift municipal accounting away from a focus that was limited to current assets and liabilities—a working capital focus—to a focus that included all financial resources and obligations, that is, both current and noncurrent items. However, only minor changes were made in the existing fund structure. The revision was intended to be a stopgap measure, to be improved upon as soon as time and experience permitted.

To illustrate the point that the fund structure is unnecessarily complicated, I shall describe briefly the types of funds that are currently required by the Governmental Accounting Standards Board, pointing out that some of them correspond to funds already used in business and that others are unnecessary.

General Fund. The General Fund accounts for the flow and status of all financial resources except those required to be accounted for in another fund. It therefore is the closest approximation to the account structure used in a business.

Special Revenue Funds. Special Revenue Funds account for the proceeds of revenues whose use is restricted to expenditures for specified operating purposes. (In other nonprofit organizations, similar funds are called "Restricted Current Funds.") Although useful for internal control, information about the source of the inflows and the uses made of them that is necessary for general-purpose financial reports could be conveyed by appropriate identification of items in the General Fund.

For example, assume that collections from parking meters are restricted to the maintenance of roads and that parking-meter revenues are therefore accounted for in a Special Revenue Fund. This fund is unnecessary. An item in the operating statement could identify the amount of parking-meter revenue. The principal asset item is cash, which is in fact mingled with other operating cash, and no important purpose is served by showing parking-meter cash separately from other cash. If not all parking-meter revenues are used in the current year, the unused amount would be a fund balance in current practice. It could be disclosed equally well as a liability in the General Fund because it represents an obligation to spend the stated amount for road maintenance next year. The fact that expenditures from this fund are used for road maintenance need not be reported; if they are not used for this purpose, the auditor should call attention to the misuse. The important information is the total amount spent for road maintenance, which could be reported in the General Fund. Dividing this amount into restricted and unrestricted portions tends to draw attention away from the total.

Capital Projects Funds. Capital Projects Funds account for resources that are to be used for acquiring or constructing major capital items. These resources are typically obtained either from borrowing or from a capital appropriation or grant from another government organization. These inflows are recorded as assets (cash) of the fund, with a corresponding credit to "revenues and other financing sources." (Note that the term "revenue" is a misnomer for inflows derived from borrowing; borrowing does not produce revenue.) As costs are incurred, the cash is used up. When the project is completed, any remaining cash is transferred to some other fund, usually to the Debt Service Fund.

Capital Projects Funds have some resemblance to the Construction Work in Progress (CWIP) account that a business uses to account for construction of fixed assets. In a business, however, borrowed funds create a liability, the cash received is recorded in the cash account, and as costs are incurred, cash is used to pay for them, with an offsetting debit to the CWIP account. When the project is completed, the total cost is transferred to a fixed asset account.

In government accounting, the Capital Projects Fund is reduced to zero when the project is completed. There is no asset to be transferred. This peculiarity arises because in a system that focuses on current assets and current liabilities, there is no way of recording long-term borrowings as liabilities. Thus, the amount borrowed is eventually offset by expenditures for constructing the asset. Furthermore, at any time during the project, the equity in the Capital Projects Fund is, essentially, the amount not yet spent for the project, whereas the balance in the CWIP account is the opposite: it is the amount spent to date on the project. This is one of the reasons why people have difficulty in understanding government financial statements.

Government organizations could use a CWIP account. If the project is financed partly by operating resources and partly by capital contributions, the construction work nevertheless needs to be managed as a single project, so a single CWIP account should be established. Contributed cash would be transferred to operating cash as the need arose. When the project was completed, the amount financed by operating resources would be reported as a fixed asset in the General Fund, and the amount financed by capital contributions would be transferred back to the Contributed Capital Fund. None of these transactions affects the measurement of income.

Debt Service Funds. Debt Service Funds hold cash that is designated to pay principal and interest on long-term debt. The cash is received from two principal sources: taxes levied specifically for debt service, which are called revenues; and amounts transferred from other funds, usually the General Fund. Amounts transferred from the General Fund are expenditures from that fund. One consequence is that interest expense never appears as such in the General Fund; the expenditures from that fund lump together principal, which is repayment of a liability, and interest, which is an expense.

This system permits manipulations with the General Fund. If a large surplus is expected in a given year (which management usually doesn't want to disclose because it can lead to a demand for lower taxes and/or higher wage rates), additional amounts can be transferred to the Debt Service Fund, which reduces the General Fund surplus. Conversely, if there is a surplus in the Debt Service Fund, the transfer from the General Fund can be reduced in years when otherwise there would be a deficit.

This fund has no counterpart in business. Borrowers may require that money be set aside in a sinking fund prior to the time that payments on debt are due, but this fund is owned by a trustee, not by the organization. In business, payment of debt principal reduces the liability, and interest on debt is an expense of the period to which it relates. This is the straightforward way of reporting what has happened.

The same principle could be used in government (and in fact will be used for all debt except borrowings made to acquire fixed assets if the GASB's Exposure Draft on Measurement Focus is finalized substantially as written). Recording transfers to a Debt Service Fund as an operating expenditure is conceptually wrong. The principal portion is not an expenditure; it is a reduction in a liability. The practice is defensible only when debt service principal is an acceptable surrogate for depreciation.

Enterprise Funds. Enterprise Funds account for activities in which revenues from the sale of goods and services are expected to finance expenses. Such activities are therefore similar to business activities. The accounting principles used for Enterprise Funds are the same as the accounting principles used in business. Accounts for Enterprise Fund activities cannot be combined with those for General Fund activities so as to provide an operating statement and balance sheet for the whole organization because the General Fund currently uses quite different accounting principles than those used for the Enterprises Funds. In particular, the General Fund records expenditures rather than expenses, and it records only transactions that affect working capital. If the GASB's Measurement Focus Exposure Draft is accepted, these differences will disappear, except for depreciation, and as explained in Part 3, debt service principal payments may be an acceptable surrogate for depreciation.

Internal Service Funds. Internal Service Funds account for transactions in which one department or other organization unit provides goods or services to other government units on a cost-reimbursement basis. In a business, these interdepartmental transactions are recorded by entries to and from individual cost centers or profit centers. Providing inventory items from a central inventory to using organizations is recorded as a credit to the inventory account of the issuing unit and a debit to an expense account of the receiving unit (or to its inventory account if the items are not consumed in the near future). Services are recorded as a credit to the service center that furnishes the service and as a debit to the organization unit that receives the service. There is no need, either in government or in business, for a report of these transactions in the general-purpose financial statements, although a separate fund may be useful as an internal control mechanism.

Trust and Agency Funds. These funds account for assets held by a government unit acting as trustee or agent. They are subdivided into four categories: expendable trust funds, nonexpendable trust funds, pension funds, and agency funds. Each is described below.

Expendable Trust Funds account for money or other assets that are received by the entity for use for a specified purpose. These assets are held in the fund until they are used for the specified purpose. At that time, they are transferred to the appropriate expense or asset account. In a business, the debit for the assets received is matched by a credit to a liability account, and the liability is discharged when costs are incurred for the specified purpose. The same procedure could be used in government. The Expendable Trust Fund mechanism may be useful for internal control purposes, but it is not necessary for financial reporting.

Nonexpendable Trust Funds are endowment. As explained in Part 3, the endowment corpus must be held intact, and the earnings on the corpus are operating revenues of the current period (unless the terms of the endowment specify otherwise). Endowment is, of course, rare in a business, but it is common in nonbusiness organizations of all types. Accounting for endowment transactions in a separate fund is a legal requirement and is also necessary for control purposes. In the language used in this monograph, nonexpendable trust funds are contributed capital.

Pension Trust Funds are not legally a part of the organization's assets in either a business or a nonbusiness organization. They are owned by the pension fund trustee, not by the organization, and pension fund assets legally cannot be mingled with the organization's assets. In a business, therefore, pension fund accounts do not appear on the financial statements, although the status of the fund is reported in Notes to the financial statements. In government, they are reported as if they were assets of the organization, although recording the assets in a separate fund accomplishes the same objective as the separation in business. A pension fund is therefore appropriate, but reporting its assets as if they were assets of the government organization is incorrect.

Agency Funds are funds that belong to an outside party, and the organization acts as an agent for that party. The organization does not own these funds. Agency Funds reflect this separation, in both business and government organizations. The difference is that governments report these funds as part of their financial statements; businesses do not. Government reporting leaves the impression that these funds are part of the government entity, which is not the case. (In both business and government organizations, minor amounts that are technically Agency Funds, such as taxes withheld from employees, are counted with other current liabilities, rather than being accounted for in separate funds.)

General Fixed Asset Account Group. As I noted in Part 1, government accounting traditionally was limited to current assets and current liabilities. In the 1960s, the National Government Accountants Association attempted to broaden the coverage, but it could not find a way of fitting noncurrent assets and liabilities into the existing accounting structure. Rather than developing a different structure, it dealt with this problem by setting up two "account groups," one for fixed assets and the other for long-term debt. These account groups are not funds.

The Fixed Asset Account Group contains a list of the fixed assets owned by the government organization, other than assets used for Enterprise Fund activities. (They are called "general" fixed assets to distinguish them from fixed assets owned by Enterprise Funds; fixed assets in an Enterprise Fund *are* part of the fund's assets.) Governments are permitted to omit infrastructure assets (e.g., roads, bridges, drainage systems, street lighting) from this list. There is an item on the equity side of the fund balance sheet that exactly equals the total of the assets. Whenever a change is made on the asset side, an equal change is made in the equity item. This account group is therefore in reality a single-entry list that is made to appear as if it were part of a double-entry accounting system by the balancing equity item. The equity item is an artificial number with no separate significance.

General Long-Term Debt Account Group. The traditional accounting structure cannot account for long-term debt. The second account group was created to provide for a listing of unpaid amounts of noncurrent debt issues. Like the Fixed Asset Account Group, it is a single-entry record, with a balancing entry labeled "amount to be provided for retirement of general long-term debt." (The fund may include other long-term obligations, such as noncurrent special assessments. If so, the asset side contains an equal amount labeled, for example, "amount to be provided from special assessments.") The offsetting amounts have no meaning of their own. In business, fixed assets are recorded as business assets, and the amounts owed to lenders, of whatever nature, are recorded as liabilities.

The GASB's Measurement Basis Exposure Draft would limit the use of account groups to fixed assets acquired with long-term borrowing and the related debt. Fixed assets acquired with currently available resources would be recorded as assets in the General Fund, and borrowings for purposes other than asset acquisitions would be recorded as liabilities of the General Fund, just as is done in business. This is a major step in the right direction.

Desirable Fund Structure

Summarizing the preceding analysis, a government organization needs (1) a fund, corresponding to the present Nonexpendable Trust Fund, to separate contributed equity and the related assets from operating equity and assets; (2) trust funds and agency funds, separate from the organization's own funds, exactly as these resources are treated in business; and (3) a general fund for all other transactions.

In general, there is need for more than one fund in any organization that has contributed equity; such a separate fund is rarely found in business because few businesses receive capital contributions. Transactions associated with capital contributions must be kept separate from transactions associated with operating activities. Separate funds are also needed to account for assets for which the organization has responsibility as trustee or agent, but which it does not own; the same requirement exists in business. These are, however, the only inherent reasons for reporting separate funds in general-purpose financial statements. The use of other funds is warranted for internal purposes if they facilitate control, but standards-setting bodies do not prescribe internal control devices.

A standards-setting body needs to prescribe a fund structure—or any other mechanical device—only to the extent necessary to meet the objectives of financial reporting and the organization's legal requirements. A fund, separate from the operating or general fund, is required to segregate contributed capital assets, liabilities, and equity from operating assets, liabilities, and equity. This is both a legal requirement and good operating practice. Even if there were no legal restriction, cash associated with contributed capital should not be used for operating purposes.

Nonbusiness organizations need to exercise detailed control over certain activities. Some prefer to use a fund mechanism for this purpose, whereas others prefer other types of accounting control. For example, one organization may prefer to set up a separate fund to control the costs incurred on capital projects, but another may decide that adequate control can be obtained by using a CWIP account together with authorization and work-order controls. Or one organization may prefer to use a working capital fund for transactions involving inventory, whereas another may prefer to run such transactions through inventory accounts in its General Fund, as is done in business. Standards setters should not dictate which alternative should be used. Any alternative that provides for adequate control and that will permit the preparation of sound financial statements should be permitted.[44]

Some people maintain that separate funds are necessary to ensure that restricted contributions, grants, and contracts are used only for the specified purpose. This is not so. Accounting controls must, of course, be in place, but these controls can be maintained within a regular account structure. For example, the Financial Accounting Foundation (FAF) must control the advance subscriptions received for each of its half-dozen or so separate publications, but the FAF does not use separate funds for this purpose. (The FAF treats these subscriptions as a business would; it disregards the "temporarily restricted" classification in Concepts Statement No. 6. Even the FAF does not find the FASB classifications useful.) Similarly, a college can control contributions earmarked for scholarships, or even for scholarships that are limited to residents of a certain state, without a separate fund structure. Even if a fund structure is used for internal control, there is no need to report its details in the financial statements.

FINANCIAL STATEMENTS

Deficiencies with Current Financial Statements

Each of the funds and account groups that I have described is listed as a separate column on the government organization's financial statements. The right-hand column on these statements shows the total of the amounts for individual funds that are listed in the other columns. It is labeled "memorandum only," which is an admission that many of the totals have absolutely no meaning. For example, the Cash item on the balance sheet includes the cash in trust and agency funds, even though this cash does not belong to the organization. The amounts earned by internal service funds for the goods and services they furnish to other departments are included on the revenue line of the operating statement, even though these are strictly internal transactions rather than revenues received from taxes, outside customers, or other external sources.

One of the peculiarities of fund accounting is that it requires "transfers" among funds. These transfers may or may not involve revenues and expenses.[45] In business accounting, all revenues and expenses are amounts of flows from and to parties that are outside the organization.

Many nonbusiness financial statements are overly complex. As pointed out in Part 2, the measurement of income is conceptually the same in both business and nonbusiness organizations.

Desirable Financial Statements

There is no inherent reason why nonbusiness organizations need to report a number of separate balance sheets and operating statements, or to fragment the information within each statement. A nonbusiness organization needs an operating statement, an operating balance sheet, an operating cash flow statement, a flow report for contributed capital, a balance sheet for contributed capital, and that is all.[46]

The *operating statement* should resemble a business income statement, with a single column of numbers, starting with revenues and ending with net income. The FASB does not specify the details of business income statements; its only specifications relate to the reporting of nonoperating items and income taxes. It does not even specify that the gross margin should be reported, although this is an extremely useful number in many companies. Standards for nonbusiness organizations should reflect a similar restraint with respect to details.

It is essential that the operating statement report on the operating performance of the whole organization. If performance reporting is fragmented into separate funds, it is easy to manipulate the report by moving amounts from and to the General Fund to and from Enterprise Funds and Debt Service Funds. As a member of the Audit Committee of the City of New York, I observed many such transactions. They conformed to generally accepted accounting principles as stated by the GASB, so technically they were correct and I could not insist that they be handled otherwise. Nevertheless, they resulted in misleading information about New York's financial performance.

As is the case with business, the overall operating statement can be supplemented by reports on individual segments. This practice is especially useful for a government organization that conducts both governmental and businesslike activities. Currently, governmental activities are reported separately from businesslike activities because different accounting principles are used for the two types of activities, so different that the separate reports cannot be combined into a single report for the organization as a whole. There should be an overall report for the whole government entity, and it should be supplemented by reports on segments.

The operating statement should not be fragmented into separate columns for restricted and unrestricted items. Such a format is both confusing and unnecessary. Showing the amount of scholarship aid coming from unrestricted sources separately from that coming from restricted resources diverts attention from the main focus, the total amount of scholarship aid.

The operating **balance sheet** should be similar to that found in business. Business standards have only a few specific requirements. For example, current assets and liabilities must be reported separately from noncurrent assets and liabilities. Nonbusiness standards should be equally general.

The **cash flow statement** should also be similar to the statement that is required in business, as described in FASB Statement No. 95.[47]

In short, neither the FASB nor the GASB should specify the format of the financial statements relating to the operating activities of nonbusiness organizations; existing standards suffice.

A separate **contributed capital** balance sheet and flow statement is necessary if the organization has significant amounts of contributed capital. This flow statement is not an operating statement; it reports inflows and outflows of contributed capital during the period, just as a similar report for a business reports inflows and outflows of equity capital. These flows should not be labeled "revenues" and "expenses"; these terms should be used only in the operating statement. The FASB and the GASB should develop standards for these balance sheets and flow statements because existing standards are not entirely applicable.

CONCLUSION

Both business and nonbusiness organizations have funds. There is only one special requirement for funds in nonbusiness organizations: separate funds are necessary to distinguish the status and flow of contributed capital from the status and flow of operating items.

Accordingly, there is only one special requirement for nonbusiness financial statements. If a nonbusiness organization has significant amounts of contributed capital, it should prepare separate statements that report the status and flows of this capital. In other respects, operating statements, balance sheets, and cash flow statements in both business and nonbusiness organizations should be prepared according to a single set of standards.

5

Implications

IMPLICATIONS FOR STANDARDS

The preceding analysis leads me to the following conclusions about present and proposed pronouncements of the Financial Accounting Standards Board and the Governmental Accounting Standards Board and about the standards-setting process.

FASB Standard on Nonprofit Organizations

The FASB should publish a standard relating to the few issues that are relevant to nonprofit organizations. The standard should focus on contributions, including related topics like the measurement of endowment income and the recognition of pledges. Material prepared by the AICPA Task Force on "display" should provide a good starting point for the development of this standard. There is no need for a standard on display; matters of display involve more details than are appropriate for a standard.

FASB Statement No. 93

This statement requires that almost all tangible fixed assets be depreciated. It should be modified to limit the requirement to assets acquired with operating resources (either available funds or borrowed funds). Depreciation on contributed capital assets should be optional. If an organization decides that such depreciation is worthwhile, the amount of expense reported on the operating statement should be offset by an equal amount of revenue.

FASB Concepts Statements

FASB Concepts Statements No. 4 and No. 6 should be revised. The unnecessary terminology developed for nonbusiness organizations and the lengthy and largely irrelevant description of the differences between business and nonbusiness organizations should be eliminated. The distinction among unrestricted, temporarily restricted, and permanently restricted contributions should be replaced by a distinction between operating contributions and capital contributions. Alternatively, since concepts statements do not have the force of standards, and since few accountants are guided by them, these statements could be left alone but no longer referred to, in the hope that they will gradually fade into oblivion. The distinction between operating contributions and capital contributions could then be covered in the nonbusiness standard referred to above.

AICPA Audit Guides

The Audit Guides for colleges and universities, health and welfare organizations, and "other" nonprofit organizations (i.e., those included in Statement of Position 78-10) should be revised so that they are consistent with the standards described in this monograph. The Hospital Audit Guide (which is under revision as a "health care" guide) should continue as a separate publication; it is not limited to nonprofit hospitals. Alternatively, the AICPA might reduce the number of separate "industry standards" and permit industry associations to perform this task. The industry guides must be entirely consistent with generally accepted accounting principles.

GASB Standards

A GASB standard on Measurement Focus should be issued that is substantially the same as the Exposure Draft of December 15, 1987, except that (1) depreciation on assets acquired with operating resources should be required, and (2) references to the fund structure should be greatly simplified. Debt service principal should be permitted as a surrogate for depreciation if, but only if, it has substantially the same effect on the measurement of income.

If a standard on capital assets is required, it should be entirely consistent with the Measurement Focus standard.

Assuming that the FASB treats depreciation as suggested above, GASB Statement No. 8, stating that state and local governmental organizations need not comply with FASB Statement No. 93, should be withdrawn.

The Standards-Setting Process

The motivation for the creation of a separate Governmental Accounting Standards Board was primarily political. Advocates maintained that government accountants would not accept some of the standards developed by the Financial Accounting Standards Board because the FASB did not understand the special requirements of government accounting. The FASB's unfortunate pronouncements on nonbusiness accounting indicate that the advocates probably were correct. Moreover, the GASB has moved rapidly to bring government accounting into the twentieth century and probably will do so before the century ends.

Although the GASB deserves high marks for its work to date, the time is not far off when its mission of reforming government accounting will have been completed. At that time, the separate Board should be discontinued—not to save money, but rather to prevent the development of separate standards for similar transactions. Already, the GASB and the FASB have arrived at somewhat different conclusions on pension accounting and on debt refunding. Because in the last analysis standards are influenced by the judgment of individuals, such differences are likely to occur in the future if separate boards continue to exist. To ensure that the problems of government organizations are adequately considered, a permanent government task force should be created. It should be asked to comment on any issue that it wishes.

If the FASB does not accept one or more of its recommendations, the FASB should explain its reasons in writing, and the task force should be permitted to respond to these explanations.

The problem of conflicting standards would be even worse if one or more new boards were created. Proposals have been made for a higher education board and for a nonprofit board. The impetus for the former is dissatisfaction with the FASB's action on depreciation and its current thinking on pledges. This dissatisfaction is completely warranted, but the solution is to convince the FASB to modify its current pronouncements, not to create a new board. A nonprofit board implies that there are major differences between accounting in business and nonprofit organizations. As I demonstrated in Parts 2 and 3, there is only one significant difference: paid-in capital in business and contributed capital in nonprofits.

The health care industry is the largest nonprofit industry. It consists of hospitals, professional associations, nursing homes, and other health care organizations. Some are for-profit, others are public nonprofit, and still others are private nonprofit. The industry is guided by a single Audit Guide, which is consistent with generally accepted accounting principles. This should be the direction of accounting developments for other industries, not the creation of a Nonprofit Accounting Standards Board.

IMPLICATIONS FOR EDUCATION

The typical course on government and/or nonprofit accounting is fragmented into sections. Perhaps three-quarters of the course is devoted to municipal accounting, and the balance consists of one or a few classes on the federal government and other nonprofit industries: colleges and universities, hospitals, charitable organizations, and "other." Discussion of individual industries is the only feasible approach because many accounting practices do not apply to nonprofit organizations in general. Moreover, many industry practices are inconsistent with generally accepted principles for business accounting, which the student has studied in introductory accounting courses.

Such a course is difficult for students for several reasons. First, they must learn the details applicable to each nonbusiness industry. Second, they have learned in introductory courses that certain principles are sound accounting, and they now find that nonbusiness organizations use different principles for the same type of transaction. Furthermore, the course typically treats fund accounting as if it were a separate branch of accounting, unrelated to business accounting. (Some courses actually have the title "Fund Accounting.") Students don't understand why fund accounting should be so different. Those who plan to take the CPA examination find out that there will surely be a question on nonbusiness accounting, so for them this course is not optional; otherwise, many would avoid it. For all these reasons, the course tends to be dull; it emphasizes memorizing details rather than learning a general set of accounting principles and applying them to specific problems.

For many instructors, the nonbusiness course is unattractive. They must learn the peculiarities of nonbusiness accounting and attempt to make sense of them for their students. This is a difficult task because the only explanation for many practices is tradition: organizations do it this way because this is the way they always have done it. Most instructors prefer a better explanation for the subject matter.

In this monograph, I have maintained that nonbusiness accounting should be the same as business accounting in most respects. Acceptance of this proposition will lead to drastically different accounting courses. Perhaps 75 percent of the minutia taught in the typical nonbusiness course will no longer be relevant. What will replace it? I see either or both of two alternatives.

One alternative is to retain a "nonbusiness" course but to use the newly available time to discuss the management uses of accounting information. There is very little time for such a discussion in the current course. Managers in various nonbusiness industries must deal with the problems that arise in their industries, and involving students in similar problems will make for a stimulating and useful learning experience. Government is the industry with the most specialized problems. A course on government that deals mostly with the management uses of accounting information, rather than with the intricacies of fund accounting, is an obvious possibility.

The other alternative is to replace the business/nonbusiness dichotomy with another way of dividing the accounting territory. One approach is to focus on service industries and to contrast them with manufacturing industries; most traditional accounting courses focus on manufacturing. For some textbooks, this would entail little more than a change in the title from "nonprofit" to "service," and a discussion of the differences between service and manufacturing organizations (e.g., the absence of work-in-process inventory as a buffer against fluctuations in demand and the resulting need to sell the services that are available each day). As I have mentioned several times, the differences between a for-profit hospital and a nonprofit hospital are trivial, and the same accounting principles apply to both. But the management of a hospital is different in important respects from the management of a factory, and the uses of accounting information are correspondingly different.

Either alternative should make for a course that is more appealing to instructors. Such a course should appeal to students as well because it would deal with an environment that interests many students as users of accounting information professionally or in volunteer work. Moreover, a focus on the uses of accounting information is more interesting than a focus on bookkeeping details.

The impetus for change will occur only if and when the specialized accounting practices in nonbusiness organizations are eliminated. This could happen quite soon, and instructors in nonbusiness accounting courses might do well to anticipate this change.

Appendix

USE AND NONUSE OF DEPRECIATION INFORMATION

As explained in Part 2, depreciation expense for assets acquired with an organization's own resources is necessary in order to measure the organization's performance in maintaining its financial capital; this is a sufficient reason for requiring it. Depreciation of assets acquired with contributed capital is not necessary for that purpose, however. A standard requiring that such depreciation be reported in general-purpose financial statements is warranted only if the benefits of doing so are worthwhile. Information about the use or nonuse of accounting depreciation provides evidence on whether users think reporting depreciation expense is worthwhile for reasons other than the measurement of the maintenance of financial capital. This Appendix reports such information.

Basis for Reimbursement

Some cost-reimbursement contracts state that book depreciation is a reimbursable cost. Organizations that have such contracts obviously should record depreciation expense. However, these contracts may or may not reimburse for depreciation expense on contributed capital assets; if they do not, this is not a reason for recording such depreciation. Moreover, contracting parties that reimburse for depreciation may also provide an alternative rule for reimbursement that is at least equally attractive. For example, the federal government will let nonprofit organizations use either straight-line depreciation or a "use allowance," which is calculated at 2 percent of the acquisition cost of buildings and improvements and 6 2/3 percent of the acquisition cost of equipment. An organization that believes it will be reimbursed for depreciation under such a contract should ascertain whether the reimbursement applies to contributed capital assets, as well as assets acquired with the organization's own resources.[48]

Similarly, the Internal Revenue Service permits depreciation expense as a deduction from revenue in calculating the taxable amount of an organization's "unrelated business income." Again, there is uncertainty as to whether depreciation on certain types of contributed capital assets is deductible. Unless such depreciation is deductible, this is not a reason for recording depreciation on contributed capital assets.

Bond Ratings

Financial institutions that issue and trade bonds and purchasers of these bonds are primary users of financial statements. They rely heavily on evaluations prepared by rating agencies. Neither of the two leading rating agencies, Standard & Poor's and Moody's, pay much attention to a depreciation number in their ratings of nonprofit borrowers. Their formula for the debt-coverage ratio, which is a key financial criterion, specifically excludes depreciation. If a borrower includes depreciation in its operating statement, the rating agency subtracts it out.[49] Most bond covenants require that the borrower maintain a specified debt-coverage ratio, and this is calculated in the same way.

Gross National Product

Gross National Product statistics, the most comprehensive data on the output of goods and services, do not include book depreciation. Instead, they report a "capital consumption allowance," which is based on estimated replacement cost and is derived from income-tax data.[50]

Cost Studies

Dozens of studies of revenues and expenses in various industries are reported annually. Most of them are prepared by industry associations for the use of their members. Some are prepared by government agencies. Many of these studies include depreciation as an item of expense. Most studies that do this are derived from data in the company's financial accounting system, in which depreciation is included as an expense, so the inclusion of depreciation is to be expected.

Even so, there may be an implicit suggestion that depreciation should be disregarded. For example, the *Quarterly Financial Report* of the U.S. Department of Commerce, which is the most massive collection of financial data of performance in various industries, gives only two expense items: "Depreciation, depletion and amortization of property, plant and equipment" and "All other operating costs and expenses."[51]

Some studies exclude depreciation; others treat it in a special way. Examples are given in the following paragraphs.

The Pannell Kerr Forster study, *Trends in the Hotel Industry*, excludes depreciation with the following explanation:

> Income after property taxes and insurance does not include deductions for depreciation, rent, interest, amortization and income taxes. Comparisons beyond income after property taxes and insurance are virtually meaningless due to wide variances in ownership, depreciation methods, financing bases, income taxes applicable, etc.[52]

The Urban Land Institute report on shopping centers has a "bottom line" labeled Net Operating Balance, which excludes depreciation. The Introduction to the study states:

Dollars and cents figures can be used to measure shopping center income to the point of the "Net Operating Balance"—that is, the amount remaining after deducting operating expenses from operating receipts but before considering depreciation, amortization of deferred costs, and financing costs. This study provides this key figure for four types of centers and for five age groups and six geographic areas for the various types.[53]

The study of condominiums, cooperatives, and planned unit developments of the Institute of Real Estate Management excludes depreciation. It has a separate schedule on capital expenditures; these are not shown on the schedule that lists expenses.[54]

The same organization makes an annual survey of income and expenses of office buildings. In this study, depreciation is also excluded.[55]

Eli Lilly and Company makes an annual study of operating statistics for chain pharmacies. It includes depreciation on equipment, but not on buildings.[56]

Laventhol & Horwarth makes an annual survey of the U.S. Lodging Industry. Its "Income Before Fixed Charges" excludes depreciation.[57]

The Building Owners & Managers Association International publishes data on income and expenses for office buildings. The data include replacement expenditures for equipment, but not depreciation on buildings.[58]

The National Restaurant Association reports on the restaurant industry. It reports "Income Before Interest and Depreciation."[59]

Comment Letters to the FASB

The Financial Accounting Standards Board received 193 letters in response to its request for comments on the Exposure Draft that became Statement No. 93 on Depreciation in Nonprofit Organizations. Of these, 22 were student reports assigned as coursework, and in 4 the respondent's attitude was not clear.

The following list divides the other 167 responses into categories, and for each category shows (a) the total responses, and (b) the percentage of respondents who indicated that depreciation on substantially all long-lived depreciable assets was not worthwhile.

	Total Responses	% Indicating Not Worthwhile
Colleges and universities	73	89%
Government organizations	15	73
Museums	11	100
Religious organizations	9	89
Independent schools	6	100
Other nonprofit organizations	6	50
Subtotal, organizations	120	87
Accounting organizations	19	42
CPA firms	15	80
Academics	7	86
Unclassified	6	50
Total	167	80%

Notes

1. In the May 1988 issue of *Accounting Education News* (p. 8), Stephen A. Zeff listed 42 academic accounting journals. Of these only one, the *Journal of Petroleum Accounting*, was related to a business.

2. The estimate of 1.2 million is made by the Internal Revenue Service. The data on the work force are from U.S. Department of Commerce, *Statistical Abstract of the United States* (Washington, D.C.: Government Printing Office, 1987).

3. I shall use the term "nonprofit"; the FASB prefers "not-for-profit." "Not-for-profit" does not even appear in *Black's Law Dictionary, Kohler's Dictionary for Accountants*, the *International Dictionary, Funk & Wagnalls Dictionary,* or the *American Heritage Dictionary.* Searches for the use of each term had the following results:

Source	Total mentions	Percent "nonprofit"
Federal court documents, pre-l980	1,687	81%
Federal court documents, 1980–85	1,703	81%
State laws, 1980–85	551	77%
Abstracts of recent articles	875	90%
Titles of books in Baker Library	57	90%

The Index of Prentice-Hall volumes on federal taxes under the entry "not-for-profit" refers to *"activities* not engaged in for profit" (e.g., hobbies). The *organizations* are referred to as "nonprofit" or "exempt."

The FASB's aversion to the term "nonprofit" is based on the naive belief that users might think the term refers to businesses that are operating at a loss.

4. Moreover, federal government accounting standards are set by the Comptroller General of the United States; the standards-setting bodies discussed in this monograph have no influence on them. These standards badly need modernizing. The General Accounting Office (GAO) has recently made certain changes and proposed others. In my opinion, however, the GAO has not addressed the essense of the problem. The GAO proposes that federal accounting be on an expense basis, which is fine; indeed, this has been a statutory requirement for more than 30 years. But the Congressional appropriations for operations are on an obligation basis. Until the Congress is willing to shift to expense-based appropriations for operations, managers are unlikely to pay much attention to the GAO's expense-based system; appropriations have the power of the purse behind them. As a former Assistant Secretary of Defense, Controller, I feel strongly about the need for expense-based appropriations, but I do not develop this point here because it would distract attention from the propositions examined in this monograph.

5. Notwithstanding the general shift to an income-statement focus (often described as the "entity" approach as contrasted with the older "proprietary" approach), the Financial Accounting Standards Board continues to emphasize the balance sheet. This has had peculiar consequences, most recently in FASB Standard 96, "Accounting for Income Taxes." Instead of estimating the effect of timing differences on income-tax expense and booking the offsetting credit or debit as a liability or an asset, this Statement focuses on the measurement of the liability and on changes in that liability as tax rates and other factors change in the future. The result is an extremely complicated practice and effects on the income statement that many regard as unsound.

6. Examples of early writings: John Allcock, *Municipal Finance for Students* (London: 1904); William

V.S. Thorpe, *Hospital Accounting and Statistics* (New York: E.P. Dutton, 1906). The Thorpe manual was adopted by all the large hospitals in New York City and by the Massachusetts General Hospital in Boston.

7. In the encumbrance basis, amounts are recorded when purchase orders are placed or salary commitments are made. This basis is still the basis of budgeting and accounting in the federal government. The term "encumbrances" has the same meaning as "obligations" or "budget authority."

8. The name of this body was changed to the National Committee on Governmental Accounting in 1951 and to the National Council on Governmental Accounting in 1976.

9. Expenditures measure the resources *acquired* during an accounting period, whereas expenses measure the resources *consumed* in the period. If an inventory item is acquired in 1988, but consumed in 1989, it is an expenditure in 1988 and an expense in 1989.

10. Much of the material in this and the following paragraphs was taken from Mary Alice Seville, "The Evolution of Voluntary Health and Welfare Accounting: 1910–1985," *The Accounting Historians Journal* (Spring 1987), pp. 57–82.

11. Material in this paragraph is taken from David J. Lyons, "Current Issues in College and University Accounting," *NACUBO Business Officer* (August 1985), pp. 18, and from Davidson, Chapter 7.

12. Relevant studies include the following:
Discussion Memorandum, "Analysis of Issues Related to the Financial Reporting Entity" (Norwalk, Conn.: Governmental Accounting Standards Board, 1988); William E. Holder, *An Empirical Study of Governmental Financial Reporting Entity Issues* (Norwalk, Conn.: Governmental Accounting Standards Board, 1987); this study is summarized in Holder's article with a similar title in *Financial Accountability and Management* (Winter 1987), pp. 311–30; Craig Shoulders, "Criteria for Identifying the Municipal Organization Reporting Entity" (Ph.D. dissertation, Texas Tech University, 1982); Craig Shoulders, "Clarification of NCGA Statement 3," *The Government Accountants Journal* (January 1984), p. 61;

James Patton et al., "An Empirical Investigation of NCGA Statement 3 on Cities' Entity Definition" (Pittsburgh: University of Pittsburgh Working Paper, 1988); John Engstrom, "The Governmental Reporting Entity," *Journal of Accounting, Auditing and Finance* (Summer 1985), pp. 305–18.

13. Paton and Littleton use the term "accomplishments" in the sense of the modern term "revenue," rather than in the sense of "net income" as used in this monograph. Most people today regard measuring accomplishments in terms of revenue as misleading, even dangerous. Many businesses have gotten into serious trouble by pursuing dollars of revenue without regard for the profitability of these revenue dollars. [W.A. Paton and A.C. Littleton, *An Introduction to Corporate Accounting Standards* (American Accounting Association Monograph No. 3, 1940), p. 15.]

14. Financial Accounting Standards Board, *Reporting of Service Efforts and Accomplishments* (1980).

As of early 1988, the Governmental Accounting Standards Board has awarded grants to 11 academics for research on program measurement of various activities. Those activities include water and sewer programs, public health, higher education, police, fire, public transit, and sanitation (GASB Action Report, February 1988). A moment's reflection about this list makes it apparent that revenues reported in general-purpose financial statements cannot report the "accomplishments" of any of these activities, with the possible exception of water and sewer programs. The research can suggest supplementary information, primarily nonmonetary, but this does not affect the financial statements.

15. *UWASIS II, A Taxonomy of Social Goals and Human Service Programs* (Alexandria, VA: United Way of America, 1976).

As another example of the diversity of information about accomplishments, see Paul D. Epstein, *Using Performance Measurement in Local Government* (New York: National Civic League Press, 1988). This 206-page book contains scores of examples of performance measures. There are many examples of efficiency measures, such as cost per mile of road paved, but I did not find a single example of a performance measure (i.e., an effectiveness or output measure) that was stated in monetary terms.

16. In my 1978 study (Anthony 1978), I devoted Chapter 2 to identifying users and their needs. I am now convinced that such an exercise is not worth much. It does not help in determining the principles that should govern the preparation of financial statements.

17. William A. Paton, *Accounting Theory—With Special Reference to the Corporate Enterprise* (Ph.D. dissertation, University of Michigan, 1922). This quotation appears on p. 253 of the Accounting Studies Press, Ltd., reprint.

18. Thomas H. Sanders, Henry R. Hatfield, and Underhill Moore, *A Statement of Accounting Principles* (New York: American Institute of Accountants, 1938), p. 25.

19. George O. May, *Accounting: A Distillation of Experience.* (New York: Macmillan, 1943), p. 215.

20. The foreign currency translation adjustment is described in FASB Statement 52. Under certain unusual circumstances, pension plan costs can be debited or credited to equity [FASB 87]. FASB 16 permits adjustments to retained earnings for (a) correction of errors, including corrections of errors in the application of accounting principles, and (b) certain income-tax transactions. A permanent decline in the market value of noncurrent marketable securities is debited directly to retained earnings [FASB 52].

21. Frequent references are made in this monograph to a concept called "maintenance of financial capital." This concept is related to the historical-cost approach to accounting. An alternative concept is called "maintenance of physical capital." It requires that historical costs be replaced by some version of current costs or replacement costs. The FASB stated: "The financial capital concept is the traditional view and is the capital maintenance concept in present financial statements" [CON 5 ¶47]. Although not specifically ruling out physical capital maintenance, none of the FASB standards relates to the physical capital maintenance concept, other than those relating to the discontinued experiment with this concept.

22. Some people do not accept my assertion that this correspondence exists, on either or both of two grounds. They say that "interperiod equity" is a short-range view that is closely linked to the long-run concept of "intergenerational equity," and that intergenerational equity is achieved only if the organization maintains its *physical* capital as contrasted with its *financial* capital. Maintenance of physical capital requires a current cost or replacement cost accounting system, and experiments with such systems in the early 1980s led to the conclusion that users of financial statements, in either business or nonbusiness organizations, do not think that such information is sufficiently reliable to be the basis for the general-purpose financial statements.

In any event, I do not believe that the GASB maintains that there is a significant difference between interperiod equity and intergenerational equity, and I agree with the GASB.

23. In general, most nonprofit organizations plan to approximately break even, that is, to operate at neither a surplus nor a deficit. This is illustrated in the following quotation by Ben Kaplan, Director of Administration of the Jewish Association for the Aged, reported in "Accounting Concerns for Nonprofit Institutions," *Corporate Accounting* (Spring 1986), p. 63.

> When we budget, we budget for needs that
> we feel really exist, and we consider a year suc-
> cessful when we spend the money doing the
> things that we are supposed to do and come in
> slightly under the budgeted deficit. Our
> philosophy is, with due apology to Dickens: In-
> come 5 pounds, expenditures 5 pounds 1 shill-
> ing—unhappy man; income 5 pounds,
> expenditures 4 pounds 19 shillings—happy man.

For a discussion of the need for profits, see David W. Young, "Nonprofits Need Surplus Too," *Harvard Business Review* (January-February 1982), p. 124.

24. Even if the equipment remains in service, its book value is zero. Accounting does not permit writing up of asset amounts when it turns out that the service life has been underestimated.

25. This conclusion does not allow for the fact that equipment expenditures probably increase from year to year because of inflation, even though the physical amounts of equipment are unchanged. As an approximation, however, the conclusion is regarded as satisfactory in understanding the financial statements because equipment typically has a relatively short life, as compared with buildings.

26. Some defend this practice on the grounds that it is consistent with the expenditure basis of accounting. This is incorrect. The payment of debt service principal is a disbursement, not an expenditure. The expenditure occurred when the asset was acquired. The payment of debt service principal is a disbursement, not an expenditure. The expenditure occurred when the asset was acquired. The payment of debt service principal is simply the use of cash to discharge a liability, just as is the case of the payment of a vendor invoice or other payable.

27. For development of this point, see Robert T. Forrester, "Should Changes in Portfolio Values Affect Operating Results?" *NACUBO Business Officer* (forthcoming).

28. These criteria are [¶67]

a. The services performed are significant and form an integral part of the efforts of the organization as it is presently constituted; the services would be performed by salaried personnel if donated or contributed services were not available for the organization to accomplish its purpose, and the organization would continue this program or activity.

b. The organization controls the employment and duties of the service donors. The organization is able to influence their activities in a way comparable to the control it would exercise over employees with similar responsibilities. This includes control over time, location, nature, and performance of donated or contributed services.

c. The organization has a clearly measurable basis for the amount to be recorded.

d. The services of the reporting organization are not principally intended for the benefit of its members. Accordingly, donated and contributed services would not normally be reported by organizations such as religious communities, professional and trade associations, labor unions, political parties, fraternal organizations, and social and country clubs.

29. The FASB has developed a new set of terms applicable to nonbusiness organizations. Instead of "equity" it uses "net assets"; for "income," "changes in net assets"; for "maintenance of financial capital," "maintenance of net assets." In some cases, the meanings are the same. In others (such as "changes in net assets"), they appear to be the same, but actually they are not. Ironically, in Concepts Statement No. 3, the FASB used "equity" rather than the more common term "owners' equity," so that its definitions would be applicable to nonbusiness organizations [CON 3 ¶143]. The drafter of Concepts Statement No. 6 disregarded this commendable effort to reduce confusion. The reason given for not using "equity" was that this term is not in common use in nonprofit organizations [fn. 26]; but "net assets" is not in common use either. The unnecessary use of new terms makes it more difficult to develop a broad statement of accounting concepts or inclusive accounting standards.

The FASB also prefers "earnings" for the bottom line, rather than the traditional "net income." "Earnings" is not an appropriate term for nonprofit organizations; "net income" is much better.

Similarly, nonprofit organizations use terms that are not used in business: "support" for a certain type of revenue; dozens of terms for the titles of financial statements and for the bottom line on the operating statement. Similar diversity of practice exists in business. The problem is probably not serious, but nonaccountants would appreciate a single name for the same construct.

30. Thomas H. Sanders, Henry R. Hatfield, and Underhill Moore, *A Statement of Accounting Principles* (New York: American Institute of Accountants, 1938), p. 1.

31. For an excellent discussion, see Most, pp. 203–24.

32. The basis of classification is discussed in the following sections of the GASB *Codification:* 1300.103, 1400, and G60.

33. I am indebted to Professor William Rotch for the idea of this diagram.

34. For a description of the effort that would be involved in appraising depreciable assets and depreciating them, see Collins and Forrester. This 159-page monograph gives a detailed description of the mechanics. The authors state: "For the vast majority of not-for-profit organizations, . . .[depreciation] will necessitate the expenditure of additional time and resources" (p. 3).

35. Several articles do not distinguish depreciation on contributed assets from other depreciation, and their authors' opinions regarding depreciation on contributed assets therefore are not discernible. Surveys also fail to make such a distinction. For example, Carl G. Ebey reported on a survey of officials in Catholic colleges and universities (in "Why Don't Colleges Depreciate Fixed Assets?" *Management Accounting* (August 1982), pp. 13–17. Of the 284 respondents, 48 percent reported that only by charging and funding depreciation could they provide for long-range maintenance of facilities. The questionnaire made no distinction between contributed assets and other assets.

36. For example, one critic set up the following situation: Suppose the organization receives a contribution of $100,000 for its endowment fund, and it earns $10,000 a year on this endowment, which it reports as operating revenue. It earmarks this $10,000 for the purchase of equipment, and 10 years later, it acquires equipment for $100,000. Is this equipment a depreciable asset, or is it in fact a contributed capital asset that, according to you, need not be depreciated? My answer is that the asset is a depreciable operating asset. The fact that its purchase can be associated with past endowment earnings is irrelevant. The $10,000 of annual earnings was recorded as operating revenue and made income $10,000 higher than it otherwise would have been. The $100,000 is a surplus resulting from the total of operating surpluses, and earmarking its accumulation in a separate fund does not change that fact. The separate fund is a segregated part of operating equity, just as a similar fund would be reported in a business. The new equipment must be depreciated in order to restore operating equity to its previous condition. If the organization decides that it no longer needs this surplus, it can deliberately operate

at a loss in the future, but this does not change the fact that it will not maintain its financial capital if it does so.

37. *Statement of Recommended Practice No. 2* of the the Accounting Standards Committee, "Accounting by Charities" (May 1988), effective in the United Kingdom and the Republic of Ireland, follows the practice recommended in IASC 20 [see ¶43]. *Exposure Draft 43* of the Accounting Standards Committee, "The Accounting Treatment of Government Grants" (June 1988), proposes to adopt IASC 20.

38. U.S. GAO Policy and Procedures Manual for Guidance of Federal Agencies, Title 2, *Accounting*: Section D20.03 (October 31, 1984).

39. An excellent analysis of the arguments regarding depreciation is James M. Fremgen, "On the Role of Depreciation in Governmental Accounting," *The Government Accountants Journal* (Winter 1985–86), pp. 10–23.

40. GASB Discussion Memorandum, "Accounting and Financial Reporting for Capital Assets of Governmental Entities" (August 31, 1987), Appendix.

41. An organization should have two budgets: an operating budget and a capital budget. The operating budget should include depreciation. The capital budget includes planned capital acquisitions and the sources of the funds to finance them. These sources include (1) depreciation, (2) a planned operating surplus, (3) operating surpluses of prior years that may specifically have been held to finance asset replacements, and (4) borrowing. Depreciation is not literally a source of funds; depreciation is a noncash expense that is added to net income to show the amount of cash flow generated by operating activities. Nevertheless, it is convenient to treat depreciation as a source of funds in analyses of this type. Depreciation is therefore a link between the operating budget and the capital budget. Including capital acquisitions in the operating budget is confusing.

42. See Standard & Poor's *Credit Week*, January 11, 1988, p. 18; and Freda S. Ackerman, Executive Vice President, Moody's Investors Service, letter to Richard F. Rosser, President, National Association of Independent Colleges and Universities, January 4, 1988.

43. Not too many years ago, the U.S. Post Office required a separate fund, with separate cash accounts, for each revenue item: first-class mail, second-class mail, rental of post office boxes, money orders, etc. This was thought to facilitate control. The trend, however, is to reduce the number of funds.

44. The FASB seems to agree that reporting by funds is not a necessary part of general-purpose external financial reporting [CON 6 ¶91, footnote]. However, it does not consider the need to separate capital transactions from operating transactions.

45. For an excellent description of the types of transfers, see Freeman and Shoulders (1983).

46. There have been a dozen field studies of user preferences for government financial reports prepared on a fund-accounting basis, compared with those prepared on a "business" basis. Most of these studies used questionnaires; in these, government accountants tended to prefer fund accounting (probably because they are accustomed to it), and other respondents tended to prefer business accounting. However, of 200 respondents to a GASB mail questionnaire sent to a variety of user groups, 82 percent stated that they found fund-accounting reports useful, and 71 percent stated that business-type reports would be useful [Jones 1985]. As is typical in questionnaire surveys, there is doubt as to whether respondents had similar interpretations of what was meant by fund-accounting and business-type reports (often stated as "fund type" vs. "consolidated" reports).

The American Institute of CPAs conducted an experiment in which 27 government entities converted their financial statements to a business basis [AICPA 1981]. Sixteen of these entities stated that they preferred the business basis, and eleven preferred the fund-accounting basis.

In a recent study, Daniels presented two sets of financial statements for the same cities to three types of user groups [Daniels 1988]. Half the subjects received the actual statements, and the other half received statements converted to a business basis. Legislators/oversight bodies had a statistically significant preference for business-basis statements. For the other two user groups, investors/creditors, and citizens (i.e., members of local political committees), there was no significant difference in the responses.

John H. Engstrom asked respondents to rank 75 items of financial information about colleges and universities in terms of their importance. Depreciation expense was ranked number 71, and accumulated depreciation was ranked number 73. These results are reported on p. 79 of his research report, *Information Needs of College and University Financial Decision Makers* (Norwalk, Conn.: Governmental Accounting Standards Board, 1988).

47. Unfortunately, the details of the cash flow statement prescribed in FASB Statement No. 95 do not fit the characteristics of many organizations, business as well as nonbusiness. It is therefore not surprising that the GASB is considering an alternative. Financial institutions also would like to have a different format.

48. U.S. Office of Management and Budget, *Circular A-122*, "Cost Principles for Nonprofit Organizations" (1980), Attachment B, Section 9.

OMB Circular A-21, "Cost Principles for Educational Institutions" has a similar provision. For information on the magnitude of depreciation in research universities, see Stanford University, *1986–1987 Decanal Indirect Cost Study* (1988). Part IV of this study compares the experience of 25 leading research universities. Part V gives information on depreciation and on the sources of funds for capital acquisitions at Stanford.

49. Standard & Poor's Corporation, *Standard & Poor's Ratings Guide* (New York: McGraw-Hill, 1979); Wade S. Smith, *The Appraisal of Municipal Credit Risk* (New York: Moody's Investors Service, Inc., 1979).

50. *Statistical Abstract of the United States* (annual), Introduction to Section 14.

51. U.S. Department of Commerce, *Quarterly Financial Report*, tables on income statements.

52. Pannell Kerr Forster, *Trends in the Hotel Industry, USA Edition* (Houston: Pannell Kerr Forster, annual) glossary section.

53. The Urban Land Institute, *Dollars & Cents of Shopping Centers: 1987* (Washington, D.C.: The Urban Land Institute, 1987).

54. Institute of Real Estate Management, *Expense Analysis: Condominiums, Cooperatives, and Planned Unit Developments* (Chicago: National Association of Realtors, annual).

55. Institute of Real Estate Management, *Income/Expense Analysis: Office Buildings, Downtown and Suburban* (Chicago: National Association of Realtors, annual).

56. *NACDS/Lilly Statistical Digest* (annual), Eli Lilly and Company.

57. Laventhol & Horwarth, *U.S. Lodging Industry* (Philadelphia: Laventhol & Horwarth, annual), introductory section.

58. Building Owners & Managers Association International, *BOMA Experience Exchange Report* (Washington, D.C.: BOMA, annual).

59. National Restaurant Association, *Restaurant Industry Operations Report* (annual).

References

(Material in brackets is a short form of reference)

AMERICAN INSTITUTE OF CERTIFIED PUBLIC ACCOUNTANTS

Accounting Principles Board [APB]

Statement No. 4, "Basic Concepts and Accounting Principles Underlying Financial Statements of Business Enterprises" (October 1970). [APS 4]

Opinion No. 9, "Reporting the Results of Operations" (December 1966). [APB 9]

Opinion No. 29, "Accounting for Nonmonetary Transactions" (May 1979). [APB 29]

Opinion No. 30, "Reporting the Results of Operations" (June 1973). [APB 30]

Accounting Research Bulletin 43 (June 1953). [ARB 43]

State and Local Government Accounting Committee, "Accounting and Financial Reporting by State and Local Governments: An Experiment" (1981).

Statement of Position 78-10, "Accounting Principles and Reporting Practices for Certain Nonprofit Organizations" (December 31, 1978). [SOP 78-10]

Industry Audit Guide, "Audits of Colleges and Universities" (1975).

Industry Audit Guide, "Audits of Voluntary Health and Welfare Organizations" (1974).

Industry Audit Guide, "Hospital Audit Guide" (1972).

Anthony, Robert N. *Financial Accounting in Nonbusiness Organizations: An Exploratory Study of Conceptual Issues.* Stamford, Conn.: Financial Accounting Standards Board, 1978.

Chatfield, Michael. *A History of Accounting Thought.* Huntington, N.Y.: Robert E. Krieger Publishing Company, 1977.

Collins, Stephen J., and Robert J. Forrester. *Recognition of Depreciation in Not-for-Profit Organizations.* Washington, D.C.: National Association of College and University Business Officers, 1988.

Daniels, Janet DeLucca. "An Investigation of Municipal Financial Report Format, User Preference, and Decision Making." DBA dissertation, Boston University Graduate School of Management, 1988.

Davidson, Sidney et al. *Financial Reporting by State and Local Government Units.* Chicago: Center for Management of Public and Nonprofit Enterprise of the University of Chicago, 1977.

FINANCIAL ACCOUNTING STANDARDS BOARD

Statements of Financial Accounting Concepts:

1. *Objectives of Financial Reporting by Business Enterprises* (November 1978). [CON 1]

2. *Qualitative Characteristics of Accounting Information* (May 1980). [CON 2]

3. *Elements of Financial Statements of Business Enterprises* (December 1980). (Superseded by Concepts Statement 6.) [CON 3]

4. *Objectives of Financial Reporting by Nonbusiness Organizations* (December 1980). [CON 4]

5. *Recognition and Measurement of Financial Statements of Business Enterprises* (December 1984). [CON 5]

6. *Elements of Financial Statements* (December 1985). [CON 6]

Statements of Financial Accounting Standards: [SFAS]

32. *Specialized Accounting and Reporting Principles and Practices in AICPA Statements of Position and Guides on Accounting and Auditing Matters* (September 1979). [FAS 32]

93. *Recognition of Depreciation by Not-for-Profit Organizations* (August 1987). [FAS 93]

Freeman, Robert J., and Craig Shoulders. "Mastering the Interfund Maze." *The Government Accountants Journal* (Spring 1983), pp. 32–44.

Governmental Accounting Standards Board (Norwalk, Conn.)

Codification of Governmental Accounting and Financial Reporting Standards. [GASB Cod. Sec.]

Statement No. 8, "Applicability of FASB Statement No. 93, Recognition of Depreciation by Not-for-Profit Organizations, to Certain State and Local Governmental Organizations" (January 1988).

Measurement Focus and Basis of Accounting—Governmental Funds (Exposure Draft, December 1987).

Hendriksen, Eldon S. *Accounting Theory.* Homewood, Ill.: Irwin, 1982.

Holder, William W. *An Empirical Study of Governmental Financial Reporting Organization Issues.* Norwalk, Conn.: Governmental Accounting Standards Board, October 1987. This study is summarized in Holder's article with a similar title in *Financial Accountability and Management* (Winter 1987), pp. 311–30.

International Accounting Standards Committee (41 Kingsway, London WC2B6YU) *International Accounting Standards*

20. "Accounting for Government Grants and Disclosure of Government Assistance." [IAS 20]

Jones, David B. *The Needs of Users of Governmental Financial Reports.* Norwalk, Conn.: Governmental Accounting Standards Board, 1985.

Most, Kenneth S. *Accounting Theory.* 2d. ed. Columbus, Ohio: Grid Publishing, Inc. 1982.

Olson, Stevan K., and Jacop R. Wambsganns. "Depreciation for Colleges and Universities: Is It Useful Information?" *The Government Accountants Journal* (Winter 1987–88), pp. 14–18.